Setting Sun

The End Of U.S. Economic Dominance

BRANDON ADAMS

Copyright © 2013 Bandon Adams

All rights reserved.

ISBN-13: 978-1482553291

CONTENTS

	Preface: Defining the Terms of Battle	1
1	Twin Deficits	13
2	Fiat Currency and the Temptations of Seigniorage	33
3	A Strange Symbiosis	51
4	Demographics and the Entitlement Crisis	67
5	The Economic Significance of Cultural Decline	79
6	The Perils of Redistribution	89
7	The Macroeconomics of Deleveraging	103
	Acknowledgments	117
	Bibliography	118

PREFACE: DEFINING THE TERMS OF BATTLE

Well, here we are. We have, on the one side, the perennially tan John Boehner, and, on the other, the scarily composed and cosmopolitan figure of Barack Obama. That the sides—conservative and progressive—decided to engage one another was no shocking surprise. What was shocking was the subject of the engagement: whether or not the US government should continue to meet its financial obligations.

The rest of the world held itself in extended disbelief as it observed, in late summer 2011, the so-called debt ceiling debate. In the eyes of the world, the United States received a lot of free passes. It was generally assumed that the people at the helm knew what they were doing. But this debt ceiling debate was something new; it was as if you were teaching your child to drive, and then, just after you'd become comfortable with him at the wheel, he took it upon himself to use the shoulder of the interstate as a passing lane.

The debt ceiling had never been taken seriously before; raising the debt ceiling had historically been regarded as a formality. If a husband and wife together agree on a budget of, say, $6,000 per month, and their after-tax income is $5,000 per month, they should not spend much time bemoaning the fact that their debt went up by $1,000 at the end of the month. A vote on the budget is implicitly a vote on the cumulative debt.

The entire debt ceiling debate took place in a cloud of confusion. For starters, members of the Republican Party routinely made the case that without dramatic action, the United States might soon go broke. In fact, the prospect that you might go broke in the future is no good reason to declare yourself broke now. No matter how dire the situation, it is almost always best to present yourself as imminently solvent.

Then there was the fact that, as the monopoly issuer of US dollars, the US government could never run out of money. When all of your debts and all of your expenses are in dollars, and you can print dollars, there are risks, but it is, on the whole, a good situation.

The Tea Party brought a battle to Washington that is about both the nation's economy and the nation's culture. There is nothing too new in the broad outlines of the fight—cultural conservatism versus progressivism; hard money versus soft money; budget austerity versus government profligacy.

The truth of the US economic situation is complicated and ugly; conflict will be an inherent part of our future economic and political landscape. The two most important fault lines are distributional—poor versus rich—and generational: young versus old. How we solve those problems will be the big story of the next twenty years, and the solutions will constitute a painful revision of the American template.

Our story starts over a half century ago. As World War II raged, 730 delegates from 44 Allied nations converged on Bretton Woods, New Hampshire, and came about as close as you come to creating an entire international economic and financial order from scratch. Most of our contemporary economic history can be related to that event.

In our Age of Twitter, success in getting together an economic summit of this type would have to be regarded as an extreme improbability. If it happened, delegates would likely be so distracted by their BlackBerrys and the twenty-four-hour news cycle as to make detailed discussion of complex, conflict-ridden economic matters impossible. We'd be lucky if we could avoid pictures of politicians playing games on their computers or, worse, browsing for prostitutes on their Ipads, as MP Simeone Di Cagno Abbrescia was caught doing during a February 2011 session in Italy's Parliament.

During the first three weeks of 1944, the attitude was somber, and the task at hand was seen as both achievable and absolutely essential. The intellects involved were exceptionally high-wattage, and they were matched with strong wills and sometimes fiery personalities. Every man in attendance—and yes, unfortunately, of the 730 delegates, all were men—had been shaped by the great tragedies of the first half of the twentieth century: World War I, the Great Depression, and World War II. The Great Depression spurred these men to deeply consider the core problems of macroeconomics from every angle. The man among the delegates with the most cultivated intellect, the sharpest mind, the quickest tongue, and the deepest experience in matters of economic policy was the great economist John Maynard Keynes.

Keynes had attended the Versailles Conference in 1919 and was so dismayed by the resulting peace settlement that he returned home and quickly penned *The Economic Consequences of the Peace*, which blasted the

"Carthaginian Peace" of Versailles and ended with the line, "But who can say how much is endurable, or in what direction men will seek at last to escape from their misfortunes?"

The first chapter of this book evaluates the sustainability of the US current account and budget deficits. Discussions of the evolution of current accounts and budget deficits figured prominently in the Bretton Woods conference; they figured strongly in negotiations of the Maastrict Treaty, the founding document of the European Union; they figure strongly in today's macroeconomic discussions; indeed, they figure strongly in *any* macroeconomic discussion. They are, simply, where you must start in evaluating the performance of a nation's economy. Current account, budget deficit, inflation rate, income and wealth distribution, national well-being as proxied for by gross domestic product—those numbers give you pretty much the whole story of a nation's economy.

Chapter 2 considers the US dollar from the perspective of the broader history of fiat, or faith-based, currency. Gold was long considered the perfect unit because its supply increased at a steady rate of about 2 percent a year, which corresponds very roughly to the rate of long-term real economic growth.[1] Bretton Woods created a system of paper currencies, backed by gold. Now we have a system of unbacked paper currencies that is tilted, for reasons we will explore, in favor of the United States. In today's world of democracy, debt, unbacked paper currencies, and free-floating exchange rates, Keynes would say that times of stability would have to be counted as the exception.

In chapter 2, we spend a bit of time exploring de Gaulle. De Gaulle's demand, in 1965, that the United States exchange the $150 million of

---

[1] T. D. Kelly and G. R. Matos, "US Geological Survey: Gold Statistics," Historical Statistics for Mineral and Material Commodities in the United States: US Geological Survey Data Series 140 (2008), http://pubs.usgs.gov/ds/2005/140/gold.pdf (accessed March 8, 2009).

French reserves for gold was the beginning of the end for the Bretton Woods system. It also marked the beginning, for de Gaulle, of a long and aggressive public relations campaign, whereby he set forth a world vision entirely at odds with the vision presented by Keynes. Whereas Keynes favored paper money and national sovereignty, de Gaulle pushed aggressively toward European integration and away from paper money. De Gaulle was clearly the key early figure in the march toward the European Union.

De Gaulle wanted gold to be at the center of human monetary relations. His arguments were not intellectual in the way that Keynes's were. Rather, he instinctively trusted gold in a way that he could never trust paper money. De Gaulle had a largely cynical view of human affairs, and he essentially felt that humans could not be trusted with the management of paper money. We will explore the cultural roots of this belief; it is a particularly French view. At one point, over a fifth of all private gold holdings were held by French individuals. In the United States, this carries over to the heavily French-influenced city of New Orleans; the biggest gold coin dealer in the country, Blanchard, is based in New Orleans, and New Orleanians are large private holders of gold. In New Orleans, there is even an active market in the fake gold doubloons that were thrown from floats in early Mardi Gras parades.

Chapter 3 looks at our symbiotic relationship with the Chinese. They provide us with an endless supply of low-cost and sometimes high-quality products, and in return we give them increasingly dubious IOUs, mostly in the form of US Treasury bonds. Analysts are sharply divided on the sustainability of the current US-Chinese economic relationship. I think about it in simple terms. There was a popular 2002 comedy called *Van Wilder*. The title character had been in college for seven years. He has a full-time personal assistant and travels around campus on a golf cart. He spends half of his waking hours chasing girls and the other half in random recreational pursuits. If an outsider wanted to know how long this arrangement could last, he should not ask Van Wilder. He should ask his dad. The creditor can provide funds to the debtor without limit.

As Americans, we relish our Van Wilder role. In January 2009, Chinese premier Wen Jiabao gave a speech at the World Economic Forum in Davos rebuking the United States for financial irresponsibility, citing "inappropriate macroeconomic policies of some economies and their unsustainable model of development characterized by prolonged low savings and high consumption."[2] Soon after this speech, President Obama announced a budget entailing a projected 2009 deficit of $1.8 trillion.[3] A budget of this magnitude—$1.8 trillion on $3.55 trillion in total spending—was entirely new and worrisome territory. It was the first time that the United States had ever had a budget deficit that exceeded 40 percent of federal spending. In *Monetary Regimes and Inflation*, Peter Bernholz suggests that, empirically, governments that exceed this threshold have a greatly enhanced risk of tipping into hyperinflation.

In his 2011 State of the Union speech, President Obama suggested that the United States should focus on developing its export capabilities. Trade imbalances of the sort that have developed between China and the United States would have been simply impossible under the Bretton Woods system, because the surplus country would see a continuous increase in the value of its currency. It was Keynes's view that if persistent trade

---

[2] Wen Jiabao, "Strengthen Confidence and Work Together for a New Round of World Economic Growth," paper presented at the World Economic Forum 2009, Davos, Switzerland, January 28, 2009, http://online.wsj.com/public/resources/documents/WenJiabao01282009.pdf (accessed March 7, 2009).

[3] Budget of the United States Government: Fiscal Year 2010, Office of Management and Budget, Summary Tables, Table S-2,
http://www.whitehouse.gov/omb/assets/fy2010_new_era/Summary_Tables2.pdf (accessed March 7, 2009).

imbalances developed and they were not easily rectified by a change in exchange rate, then the onus of restoring balance should be shared by the surplus country and the deficit country. In the modern instance, Keynes would say that Chinese policymakers should do what they can to encourage an increase in the level of purchases of US goods and services, in an effort to restore trade balance. Keynes believed that forcing the deficit country to bear the full burden of the adjustment tended to be deflationary and that it tended to provoke an anti-trade political backlash. Shifting some of the burden to the surplus country tended to be more conducive to world trade and tended to provide for a much quicker adjustment period.

Obama's stance on the 2009 budget was the first evidence of political naïveté with regard to budget issues. In early 2009, Obama had the political capital to run monstrous deficits for as long as he wanted. Instead of taking advantage of this political capital, he set the world up for disappointment and put himself in a can't-win scenario.

The Obama administration projected that real economic growth in 2010, 2011, and 2012 would be 3 percent, 4 percent, and 4 percent, utterly ridiculous numbers.[4] They did this so that they could project budget deficits for 2010, 2011, and 2012 that would be substantially smaller than the projected 2009 deficit of $1.8 trillion. This fuzzy math was surely not going to fool our Chinese creditors; it did, however, disappoint voters, as deficits remained huge into 2010 and 2011.

Chapter 4 considers the gargantuan problem of our entitlement crisis. The chapter focuses on the huge federal programs: Social Security, Medicare, and Medicaid. The core problem of the crisis is that we need these programs (private pensions and private savings are insufficient by far for most Americans), yet we won't be able to support them at anything

---

[4] Budget of the United States Government: Fiscal Year 2010, Table S-8.

close to current benefit levels as the population ages. The unfunded liabilities of these programs have been estimated at $52 trillion.[5]

The reform of our entitlement programs will be central to the revision of the American template that this book suggests must occur. The fight over how these reforms will take place, and when, will be key elements in the massive generational tension that awaits us in upcoming decades. Our discussion of budget deficits and current accounts begins in chapter 2, but it is in chapter 4 that the nightmarish dimensions of the long-term US fiscal outlook are really spelled out. The problems will reach the height of their severity two or three decades from now, but, even in the current decade, it will be difficult to lower budget deficits without making some headway toward entitlement reform. The aging of our population (the first Baby Boomers started collecting Social Security in 2008) and the consequent projected rise of Medicare and Social Security spending mean that the battle to lower our deficits over time is a battle that is fought steeply uphill.

Chapter 5, "The Economic Significance of Cultural Decline," is, to be sure, treacherous territory. I isolate three cultural variables—attention span, savings ethic, and societal trust levels—and speculate that declines in these areas presaged economic decline and are likely to continue to weigh on US competitiveness and perhaps even US economic and political stability. I define economic growth as a growing level of output per person, within the constraints of environmental and fiscal sustainability, and I argue that the decline in the cultural variables mentioned above has threatened our long-run growth path.

My argument with regard to attention span is that humans have chosen to live more complicated lives than ever before. This speed and complication fractures attention spans. We realize this, and yet we continue

---

[5] Laurence J. Kotlikoff and Scott Burns, The Coming Generational Storm (Cambridge, MA: MIT Press, 2004), 68.

to welcome more complication in our lives. It's unclear where this will end, but the recent banking crisis is a good preview. We created an industry of unimaginable complexity, and now that problems have arisen, we've learned that few people have even the vaguest sense of what is going on. The banking industry has never seemed more clueless. They are unable even to manage the foreclosure process—tens of thousands of houses are sitting empty across the country. Many of these houses ultimately will need to be torn down due to mildew.

I interpret "the savings ethic" very broadly as the degree to which a society is willing to sacrifice today for the benefit of tomorrow. By most measures, the United States of the twenty-first century is not a master of deferred gratification. I introduce controversial measures into the debate—for example, I cite the increasing incidence of tattoos and the increase in obesity as evidence for the decline in the savings ethic.

"Societal trust" is defined as both the citizens' trust in their government and the trust they are willing to place in one another, and how quickly that trust is formed. I believe strongly that one of the key factors driving the dynamism of the United States' economy is high levels of trust among individuals, and trust between individuals and their governing institutions. Many of the American success stories began in a bar or at a coffee shop, where the chance meeting of two strangers quickly developed into a bond of trust, and that bond later cemented itself in a business venture. I argue that a decline in trust both on the individual and on the institutional level inhibits the vital and unique entrepreneurial aspects of our economy.

Chapter 6 considers the politics and the perils of redistribution. Politicians must consider the dual problems of growing an economy and pleasing a constituency. The latter objective often requires distributing wealth to a greater extent than would be optimal from the perspective of economic growth. There are, of course, promises as well as perils associated with redistribution. There are strong arguments for why redistribution might increase the long-term economic growth rate. Also, needless to say, there are immediate utility benefits, as those who receive money, being poorer, often appreciate the money more than the rich from whom it has been taken. The worry in any economic crisis is that economic problems will spill over into political problems. Cyclical, or even deeply structural, economic problems are not too severe a problem within the United States. We will not forget knowledge learned up to this point; our ability to produce goods and services should be mostly unaffected by crisis. The challenge is to make sure that all segments of society continue to get along through the crisis. Meeting this challenge is a political problem in which the politics of redistribution figures heavily.

Chapter 7, "The Macroeconomics of Deleveraging," tackles the extremely difficult but timely topic of the impact of debt levels on macroeconomic performance.

How we resolve the key debates of cultural conservativism versus progressivism, hard money versus soft money, and budget austerity versus government profligacy are not trivial matters. As a poker player would say, "We are playing pretty high." We might be playing for all of it. The whole enterprise seems at risk. In South Korea, the most fervent gambler will—rarely, admittedly—play heads up poker where the cost of losing is a finger. In the United States, we're somewhere between, in macroeconomic terms, playing for a finger and playing Russian roulette.

Our problems now are so severe that there is a tendency to look back ten or twenty years and think that the situation then was positively rosy by comparison. In Lorne Michaels's show *Portlandia*, one of the characters says, "The nineties are alive in Portland." Indeed, the 1990s were a relatively favorable time, but it is not as if we were, at that point, the elite athletes of the world economy. We were more akin to a fifty-year-old who is forty pounds overweight. He's more than a few decisions away from catastrophe. He can maintain his basic life patterns and still be in tolerable condition ten years down the road. He's not, however, in a great spot to pursue a bender. If he does, he might find himself a hundred pounds overweight at sixty. And you don't see many really fat seventy-year-olds.

1 TWIN DEFICITS

The United States is quickly becoming the profligate uncle of the world economy. Rather than showing the temperance and humility that is becoming of a debtor, it insists that all is fine, while hiding its financial reality whenever possible and seemingly choosing, at every step, to double down by borrowing more, consuming more, and gambling higher. Perhaps this is the fate of capitalist democracy in the modern era; since small, painful steps toward prudence are politically infeasible, democracies instead pursue aggressive policies that move them from crisis to crisis.

How did we go from being the world's largest creditor nation to being the world's largest debtor nation? Some of the answer is cultural—we're become a mostly amoral and listless people, a subject that will be explored in detail in chapter 5. Some of the answer is structural: the twin forces of globalization and technology have worked to largely destroy the middle class and make huge amounts of social spending a political necessity. Here's a situation for our time: I was having dinner with a friend in Las Vegas at one of the top-rated restaurants in the city, Raku, and was stunned to learn after the fact that he'd paid for his half with his unemployment Visa debit card. He told me that he just calls a government office every month and answers two simple questions, and then the card is refilled.

We're pretty far from The Greatest Generation. In large measure, our future fiscal debates will come down to this: Are taxpayers cool with my friend using his unemployment Visa card to pay for his $120 dinner? The dominant tools of social spending—Social Security, Medicare, Medicaid, unemployment insurance—are imprecise and combine elements of immense social value with elements of grotesque waste.

The US budget and current account deficits are closely related. The domestic economy consists of government, individuals, and businesses. When those groups choose to consume more than they collectively produce, the difference must be imported. In other words, overconsumption shows up as a current account deficit. In 2008, the US current account deficit was $706.1 billion.[6] In 2008 imports were $2.5 trillion and exports were $1.8 trillion.[8] As a slight simplification, one can imagine that $1.8 trillion of our $2.5 trillion in imports are "paid for" by our $1.8 trillion in exports, and that, for the remaining $700 billion, the world accepts IOUs from us in the forms of US assets (lately, mostly US Treasury bonds and other credit instruments).[9] The current account improved in

---

[6] "US Current Account Deficit Q4 2008," Bureau of Economic Analysis, http://www.bea.gov/newsreleases/international/transactions/2009/trans408.htm (accessed January 14, 2013).

[8] "US Trade in Goods and Services—Balance of Payment (BOP) Basis," US Census Bureau, http://www.census.gov/foreign-trade/statistics/historical/gands.pdf (accessed March 19, 2009).

[9] David Amber, "Foreign Purchases of US Debt and Equity: Some Stylized Facts," http://www12.georgetown.edu/students/dpa3/doc/bondeq_facts.pdf (accessed March 9, 2009). However, in 2009, the US current account deficit actually decreased to $419.9 billion, which is the

2009 ($419.9 billion) and stayed near that level in 2010 ($441.9 billion), 2011 ($465.9 billion), and 2012 (~$475 billion).[10] The sum of our current account deficits over time very roughly approximates our net international investment position (NIIP). Our net international investment position is equal to foreign assets held by the United States minus US assets held by foreigners. The United States has a better net international investment position than would be suggested by summing up all of our annual current account deficits, because the return on international assets held by the US has generally been much better than the performance of US assets held by foreignes.

The best way to tell the story of our so-called twin deficits is in snapshots. Our first snapshot is January 1965, the first time that the Bretton Woods "gold window" was tapped; our second snapshot is August 1971, when Nixon effectively ended the Bretton Woods system; and the third snapshot is August 2011, the month when the US Congress refused to increase the legislative ceiling on the national debt until the last possible moment.

The international economic system designed at Bretton Woods was a trading system anchored in gold. The US dollar was fixed to gold at a rate of $35 an ounce, and the United States stood ready to buy gold from any government at this rate. Policymakers of the time used their best judgment to set all other exchange rates; these exchange rates would then be allowed to fluctuate within tight bands. Thus all exchange rates were fixed against the dollar, whose price was in turn fixed against gold. By today's standards,

---

smallest current account deficit since 2001. The explanation for this decrease is a fall-off in demand for foreign goods. For more information, see: "US International Transactions: Fourth Quarter and Year 2009," Bureau of Economic Analysis, March 18, 2010,
http://www.bea.gov/newsreleases/international/transactions/transnewsrelease.htm (accessed June 5, 2010).

[10] "Table 1, US International Transactions," Bureau of Economic Analysis, December 18, 2012, http://www.bea.gov/iTable/iTable.cfm?ReqID=6&step=1 (accessed January 14, 2013).

the system was fundamentally inflexible, and its continued survival required that economic actors occasionally act against their own short-term economic self-interest. It was not, to an economist's way of thinking, robust; it could not withstand a continued onslaught of selfish behavior.

Britain was the last country to ratify the Bretton Woods agreement, and it did so only after receiving a US promise of $4.4 billion in aid. Britain had sought greater protectionism than allowed for by Bretton Woods; it felt that in the immediate postwar environment, its products were not internationally competitive. The Bretton Woods system, effective as of December 6, 1945, made for a US-dominated trade regime. In high contrast to Woodrow Wilson's shrinking international role after World War I, Roosevelt, before his death in April 1945, sought to construct a world order in which the United States was the clear hegemonic power, and the Bretton Woods agreement fit nicely into this design.

Once the Bretton Woods system went into effect, there was an unstated expectation that countries should not present their dollars for gold at the gold window, although any country was entitled to do so at any point, at a rate of $35 per ounce. It was clear to all other countries that the United States could possibly abuse its new role as the reserve currency by running high trade deficits year after year. After all, in theory, if no one ever made use of the gold window, then the United States could in theory print, at no cost to itself, as many dollars as it would like each year, and then simply exchange those dollars for the goods and services of other countries. The dollars would simply pile up in the central banks of the surplus countries.

It was not hard to foresee that, should the statesmanlike attitudes that engendered the Bretton Woods agreement wear off over time, countries could, in a rush to pursue their own individual self-interest, make something like a rush on the US gold window.

Seventeen years after ratification of the Bretton Woods agreement, in 1964, the US current account deficit reached $3 billion, at the time an astonishingly high figure. This was considered a near national emergency. Among the measures seriously debated: an exit tag of $50 or $100 on all citizens leaving the United States, in an effort to discourage tourism abroad. Vastly improved jet service to the Continent encouraged upper-income Americans to spend a high fraction of their disposable income on newly accessible European vacations. President Johnson vowed, in 1965, "strong and specific" actions to deal with the US current account deficit.

The Bretton Woods construct was under no serious danger, but the writing was on the wall. It was clear that Johnson intended to pursue a policy of both guns and butter. Indeed, in retrospect, the US federal budget came unmoored around 1964 and never really looked back to the dock.[11] Due to a combination of political and economic constraints, it has proved hard to raise more than about a fifth of GDP in tax revenue at any point in our history. Despite all of the changes in tax structure we have seen, federal taxes as a share of GDP have remained fairly constant since 1950, generally staying between 17 and 20 percent of GDP. This level of revenue has proved insufficient to cover, since 1964, the Great Society and the escalation of the Vietnam War, OPEC and the federal debt-driven stagflation of the 1970s, and the 1980s military buildup of Ronald Reagan. Aside from these shocks, the baseline level of government expenditures tended to grow, driven primarily by the inertia of government programs, the rising cost of health care (affecting Medicare and Medicaid), and influence peddling in Washington, D.C. One aspect of US politics that will forever hinder the US economy is that, for a few hundred thousand dollars,

---

[11] "Historical Tables: Budget of the United States Government, Fiscal Year 2008," Office of Management and Budget, http://www.gpoaccess.gov/usbudget/fy08/pdf/hist.pdf (accessed March 20, 2009).

one may hire a lobbyist (or, God forbid, a politician) who may potentially convey benefits worth tens or hundreds of millions.

Since Bretton Woods legally obligated the United States to exchange dollars for gold at a rate of $35 an ounce, in theory the countries with whom we ran trade deficits in 1964 could have accepted payment in gold, not dollars, to the tune of $3 billion. Even if the United States' trade partners had demanded this whole sum, we would still have been left with a gold supply of over $12 billion. Yet, to the outside world, the trends were becoming clear, and it looked as if the United States might at some point unilaterally raise the exchange rate of gold from $35 an ounce to some higher level.

Into this fold stepped Charles de Gaulle, who famously said, "France has no friends, only interests." And so, despite pledging in 1963 to support the Bretton Woods system, de Gaulle converted $150 million into gold in January 1965 and another $150 million soon after. These actions encouraged Spanish dictator Francisco Franco to exchange $60 million for gold, also in early 1965. De Gaulle exhorted the rest of the world to exchange dollars for gold and to end the system of "exorbitant privilege" which, in his view, tilted the international trading regime strongly in favor of the United States.

In his bid to undermine American power, de Gaulle was unsuccessful. He was, first and foremost, a Francophile, and, secondly, a Europhile. In 1959, he declared, "Yes, it is Europe, from the Atlantic to the Urals, it is the whole of Europe that will decide the destiny of the world." He can be regarded as one of the central figures of the organization that later became the European Union. Churchill respected de Gaulle but disliked him; Roosevelt simply hated him. De Gaulle's tactics in international trade were an extension of his general strategy of taking power away from the Anglosphere and bringing it toward the Eurosphere. In this particular battle, it was the Anglosphere that triumphed. The Bretton Woods construct held as the key surplus nations of Germany, Japan, and Canada refused to heed de Gaulle's call to exchange their dollars for gold.

***

Some macroeconomic phenomena can be related to a poker game. At the start of the game, all the players have chips; if they didn't, they would not be given a seat. As the game goes on, players are protective of their chips and keen to acquire more. As long as everyone has chips and is in action, everyone is happy and the poker game operates as it's supposed to—the house takes its cut, the dealer gets some tips, the best players usually win a little, the worst players lose a little but enjoy the ride. But when one or more players run out of chips, all hell breaks loose.

Within a country—take the United States, circa 2013—what can happen is that a large number of economic participants simply run out of chips. At a minimum, this makes them unhappy; sometimes it makes them want to turn over the table and demand a restart. The international trading system is like a crooked local game where the hosts get to dictate the rules in their own favor. It's perfectly acceptable for a newbie to the system—a tourist in poker terms, a Latin American country in the international trading system—to lose all its chips, but if the established winners begin to lose, the rules are changed.

Richard Nixon was, by general agreement, the sharpest poker player to have ever been president. Poker players are terrible at any form of administration, but they are keenly sensitive to protecting their own self-interest. Nixon adopted an age-old gambling tactic: he didn't pay. In poker, there's one way to ensure victory; play and collect on the wins, but refuse to pay upon losing.

Americans have a bit of a historical blind spot about the closing of the gold window: they don't view it as a particularly bad offense. But in fact it was a theft of sorts. By 1971, the proper price of gold had moved some way from its official price of $35 an ounce, and the international community was performing a kind of service to the United States by continuing to hold dollars. Rather than make the scale of the theft explicit by, for instance, changing the conversion rate from $35 to $70, the United States chose to eliminate convertibility entirely, such that the rest of the world was left holding, not a promise to pay gold, but rather a piece of paper of potentially rapidly depreciating value. It was a move to a world of currencies propped up entirely by faith—a world of fiat currencies.

The death blow to Bretton Woods came from an entirely unlikely source: Great Britain. On August 11, 1971, Great Britain requested that $3 billion of its currency reserves be exchanged for gold at $35/ounce; this would have meant a depletion of forty thousand tons of gold bullion from the vaults of Fort Knox. John Connally, Nixon's Treasury Secretary, had earlier advised Nixon that requests at the gold window were becoming increasingly likely, and Connally was the first to suggest to Nixon that the response should be the rather extreme one of simply closing the gold window entirely.

John Connally might be thought of as the Karl Rove of his era. In *Nixonland*, Rick Perlstein writes, "One of the things that delighted Nixon was that Connally had no fixed ideology. In fact, he boasted that he had no fixed convictions about anything: 'I can play it round or I can play it flat, just tell me how to play it' was one of his favorite nostrums—paraphrasing the apocryphal applicant for a job as a rural science teacher, when asked about his convictions on the shape of the earth."[12] It was Connally who engineered the so-called Nixon Shock. The Nixon Shock, announced on national TV Sunday, August 15, 1971, immediately ended the convertibility

---

[12] Rick Perlstein, Nixonland: The Rise of a President and the Fracturing of America (New York: Scribner, 2008), 600.

of dollars into gold (the British request of August 11 was not honored), implemented a 10 percent border tax on imports and a small package of tax relief for individuals and businesses, and called for a ninety-day freeze on wages and prices.

Ending dollar convertibility was a risky and extreme move for Nixon to take. It is simply impossible to say, ex post, whether the move was beneficial for the United States as a whole. Nixon and Connally had dual objectives in mind: do what was best for the US economy, while also maximizing the chances of reelection in 1972. Connally and Nixon felt that reelection would be best served by the elimination of convertibility, as this would give the administration free rein in running large budget and current account deficits ahead of the '72 election. But eliminating convertibility might also have been in the medium-term best interests of the United States. Nixon felt that there simply wasn't time to explore the middle-ground solution of changing the dollar-gold conversion rate from $35 an ounce to some higher price. What appeared most likely to Nixon was that, if he did not end gold convertibility or change the conversion rate, the United States would see an endless run on its gold stock. So for Nixon, the choice was: end convertibility now, or run out of gold and then end convertibility.

While one can debate whether removing dollar convertibility was in the best interests of the United States, it is almost beyond dispute that it did not serve the world's interests. First, US dollar reserves held in central banks, which were previously directly convertible to gold, were now worth an entirely uncertain figure. There was a fundamental unfairness about what had happened. Countries that had run surpluses against the United States did so in the expectation that the dollar reserves they accumulated were "as good as gold." They would have much preferred to see the United States increase the rate of conversion rather than to have been faced with the end of convertibility. Nixon, in his day, had no doubt been in poker games where the bank didn't quite match up at the end of the night. In such cases, there is almost never an excess of cash in the bank. The house or the banker either eats the loss or forces the other players to accept a worse than expected exchange rate of chips for cash. What the house never does is eliminate the conversion of chips to cash entirely.

Nixon expected an international uproar after the Nixon Shock, but in fact the uproar was limited. The move had been expected and feared for some time, and, when it occurred, there was mostly resignation. The carefully planned reality of the Bretton Woods system gave way to a new reality that consisted of no planning whatsoever. What Nixon did was stand up on the world stage and say, "Okay, sorry that didn't work out. Every man for himself from now on." His imposition of an import tax only added salt to the wound. What would replace the Bretton Woods system would be the great international bazaar, where each currency floated freely against every other. Such a system has a lot going for it on efficiency grounds; it does not score quite so well in creating a climate for stability or predictability.

***

The debt ceiling debacle of August 2011 requires some historical antecedent. In 1999, the US fiscal house briefly appeared to be under control. The budget surplus in that fiscal year was $125.6 billion, coming off a surplus of $69.3 billion in fiscal year 1998.[13] Bill Clinton was an extremely competent leader, and part of this budgetary success stemmed from the fact that, during most of his tenure, the level of government expenditure grew more slowly than GDP.[14] That said, there were more

---

[13] "Historical Tables: Budget of the United States Government, Fiscal Year 2008."

[14] Compare: "Historical Tables: Budget of the United States Government, Fiscal Year 2008," and "National Income and Product Accounts Table—Table 1.1.1 Percent Change from Preceding Period

important, transitory reasons for the budget surpluses during those years. First, cyclical considerations were dominant—this was a time when the economy was running far above trend: real GDP increased by 4.5 percent, 4.2 percent, and 4.4 percent in 1997, 1998, and 1999, respectively, compared to an average rate of 3.5 percent since 1930.[15] Moreover, the stock market was booming—the NASDAQ went up 23 percent in 1997, 39 percent in 1998, and 84 percent in 1999.[16] This translated into huge capital gains tax revenues. These revenues were $84 billion in fiscal year 1998 and $99 billion in fiscal year 1999, compared to an average of $30.8 billion in 1990–1994.[17] Second, the government lumps transfer programs in with the overall budget. This serves to make the budget numbers look very good in years in which the ratio of workers to retirees is high (such as 1998 and 1999) and very bad in years in which there are few workers in relation to retirees.[18] The first of the Baby Boomers (those born between 1946 and 1964, peaking in 1957 with the birth of 4.3 million babies) were eligible for Social Security in 2008, but the worst of the problems will come around 2025.[19]

---

in Real Gross Domestic Product," Bureau of Economic Analysis, http://www.bea.gov/national/nipaweb/SelectTable.asp?Popular=Y (accessed March 18, 2009).

[15] "FRED Graph: Percent Change Real Gross Domestic Product, Annual," Federal Reserve Bank of St. Louis, http://research.stlouisfed.org/fred2/graph/?chart_type=line&s[1][id]=GDPCA&s[1][transformation]=pch (accessed July 15, 2009).

[16] Calculated from: "NASDAQ Composite," finance.yahoo.com, http://finance.yahoo.com/echarts?s=%5EIXIC#chart1:symbol=^ixic;range=my;indicator=volume;charttype=line;crosshair=on;ohlcvalues=0;logscale=on;source=undefined (accessed August 5, 2009).

[17] "Capital Gains Taxes and Federal Revenues," Congressional Budget Office, http://www.cbo.gov/doc.cfm?index=3856&type=0 (accessed March 17, 2009).

[18] Kimberley Amadeo, "US Federal Budget: Mandatory Spending," http://useconomy.about.com/od/fiscalpolicy/p/Mandatory.htm (accessed June 3, 2009).

[19] US Census Bureau, "Oldest Baby Boomers Turn 60!" http://www.census.gov/Press-Release/www/releases/archives/facts_for_features_special_editions/006105.html (accessed March 17, 2009); "The Boomer Stats," Baby Boomer Headquarters, http://www.bbhq.com/bomrstat.htm (accessed March 16, 2009).

Mao, when asked about the impact of the French Revolution, reportedly replied, "It is too early to tell." That admonition aside, I believe it's fair to judge the Bush administration's economic policies as disastrous. By the time George W. Bush took office, severe imbalances had been accumulating in the world economy for a long while, but we kicked up the pace quite a bit starting in 2001.

The dot-com bubble is one of a few contenders for the biggest financial bubble in history, the others being the Japanese bubble in real estate and equities in the late 1980s and the nearly worldwide housing bubble of 2003–2007. It's no accident that these are all recent—the tremendous and mostly immeasurable growth in global liquidity that's occurred in the last thirty-five years is the root cause. The end of the dot-com bubble can be dated fairly clearly as mid-March 2000. From March 13, 2000, to April 28, 2000, the NASDAQ fell by 27.1 percent.[20] Some remnants of the bubble remained—Enron, for example, reached an all-time high in September 2000.[21] It filed for bankruptcy on December 2, 2001.[22] The year 2002, in retrospect, looks as if it would have been a nice year to settle down a bit. Coming off the technology bubble and revelations of corporate scandal, it would have been a good year for humility.

Alas, 2002 turned out not to be the year of humility. Events were moving quickly, and in retrospect it seems that the Bush administration (which, at this time, controlled Congress to a nearly unprecedented extent)

---

[20] Numbers calculated from: "NASDAQ Composite Graph," Euroinvestor.com, http://www.euroinvestor.co.uk/stock/chart.aspx?id=325423 (accessed June 3, 2009).

[21] "The Fall of Enron Stock," Encarta, http://ca.encarta.msn.com/media_701610605/the_fall_of_enron_stock.html (accessed March 17, 2009).

[22] "Enron Corp. Bankruptcy Information," United States Bankruptcy Court: Southern District of New York, http://www.nysb.uscourts.gov/enron.html (accessed March 16, 2009).

was preoccupied with Iraq.[23] It was fairly clear in early 2002 that one economic matter that would not be tackled was the budget deficit; that was due for an explosion. President Bush and Congress cut taxes in 2001, 2002, and 2003.[24] These tax cuts were estimated to cost the government $188 billion per year.[25] This was the first example in American history of a tax cut during wartime.[26] Two weeks after September 11, 2001, President Bush urged Americans to "Get down to Disney World in Florida,"[27] and his brother Jeb, then the governor of Florida, urged them to "consider it their patriotic duty to go shopping, go to a restaurant, take a cruise, travel with their family."[28] It took a while, but Americans obliged, spurred on by Bush tax cuts and by easy monetary policy.

I'm a close observer of Alan Greenspan, chairman of the Federal Reserve during Bush's tenure, and I still don't know quite what to make of him. It's fairly clear that monetary policy was lax throughout his tenure and that, despite early hesitation (his famous "irrational exuberance" speech of December 1996), he was ultimately accommodating to both the technology bubble and the housing bubble.[29] The central banking community in the

---

[23] See Jonathan Chait, The Big Con: Crackpot Economics and the Fleecing of America (New York: Houghton Mifflin, 2007).

[24] William Ahern, "Comparing the Kennedy, Reagan and Bush Tax Cuts," Tax Foundation, http://www.taxfoundation.org/news/show/323.html (accessed March 17, 2009).

[25] Ibid.

[26] Steven A. Bank, Kirk J. Stark, and Joseph J. Thorndike, "War and Taxes" (Washington, D.C.: Urban Institute Press, 2008), 3.

[27] "Remarks by President Bush to Airline Employees, Chicago O'Hare International Airport, Chicago," http://bulk.resource.org/gpo.gov/papers/2001/2001_vol2_1172.pdf (accessed March 16, 2009).

[28] Washington Post, "Theme Parks See Crowds After Attacks," September 22, 2001.

[29] Alan Greenspan, "The Challenge of Central Banking in a Democratic Society" (paper presented at the Annual Dinner and Francis Boyer Lecture of the American Enterprise Institute for Public Policy Research, Washington, D.C., December 5, 1996). Also see George Cooper, The Origin of Financial Crises: Central Banks, Credit Bubbles and the Efficient Market Fallacy (Petersfield, Great Britain:

early years of this century was divided on whether central banks should concern themselves with asset bubbles. I'm fairly strongly convinced that they should, but identifying a bubble is a difficult and politically perilous business, and Greenspan (an acolyte of Ayn Rand, let's not forget) was philosophically disinclined to such an activist approach.[30]

Bush's tax cuts in wartime speak in part to the grotesque distortion of so-called Keynesian economics that has occurred in every country since Keynes first developed his ideas in his 1936 classic *The General Theory of Employment, Interest, and Money*.[31] Keynes urged countries to run roughly balanced budgets over time, with budget deficits in bad times countered with budget surpluses in good times. Countries distort this advice in the expected way—they cut taxes and increase expenditure in bad times, but they don't counter these measures with revenue-enhancing measures in good times. Bush's policies—tax cuts during wartime, in good times and bad, without any offsets in even the best of times—are just an extreme example of this seventy-year trend in fiscal policy.

I was not aware of how deep the misunderstandings were in this area until I listened carefully to the debates on the debt ceiling in August 2011. Many congressmen, lacking an education in economics, relate macroeconomics to household economics, when in fact the two things bear little relation to each other. Running a balanced budget or a budget surplus

---

Harriman House, 2008).

[30] For further reading, see Cooper, The Origin of Financial Crises; Harriet Rubin, "Ayn Rand's Literature of Capitalism," New York Times, September 15, 2007, http://www.nytimes.com/2007/09/15/business/15atlas.html?pagewanted=1&_r=1 (accessed March 18, 2009). Also, for Alan Greenspan's letter to the New York Times about Atlas Shrugged, see: "Letters to the Editor," New York Times, November 3, 1957, http://graphics8.nytimes.com/packages/pdf/business/20070915RAND_nyt_greenspanletter.pdf (accessed March 17, 2009).

[31] John Maynard Keynes, The General Theory of Employment, Interest, and Money (New York: Harcourt, Brace, 1936).

is a great thing as a household, but it is almost definitely a terrible policy for a country that prints its own currency and borrows in that same currency.

Republican congressmen appeared to argue that they had to pursue harsh tactics around the debt ceiling deadline in order to force the Democrats to enact sharp budget decreases over time, which, if not enacted, would cause the US government to go broke. Little did they know that the only thing that could cause the US government to go broke would be a failure to raise the debt ceiling! Let's get this straight, people: if you're the monopoly issuer of US dollars, and your debt is in US dollars, you can't go broke. You might go broke slowly, due to a decline in the purchasing power of the dollar, but going broke now to preclude the possibility of going broke in the future is not good policy.

There are only three ways that the US government can default on its debt. The first and most salient option is by failing to raise the debt ceiling. The rest of the world watched in horror as we threatened to use this technicality to commit economic suicide. The whole idea that Congress is required to increase the debt ceiling is itself ridiculous; every year, it votes on the budget, which is implicitly a vote on what will happen to the deficit (and, by implication, the debt). The second way the government could default is by choice; in some unlikely but possible future scenario, the US government might decide that defaulting on its debt, in the way that Russia defaulted on its external debt in 1998, is its best policy option. The third way that government can default is a bit obscure: since the Federal Reserve is the only entity that can create money, and yet the Treasury is the government entity that spends, taxes, and issues debt, it is theoretically possible that the Federal Reserve would refuse to be the buyer of last resort for Treasury bonds. This bizarre civil war is really just a theoretical possibility; in reality, the Federal Reserve, despite its nominal independence, is under strong influence from both the executive and legislative branches of the government, and it would be forced to buy Treasury bonds directly from the Treasury in the event that the Treasury was having difficulty selling its bonds.

Kenneth Rogoff and Carmen Reinhart, in *This Time is Different: Eight Centuries of Financial Folly*, suggest that a historical norm is for countries to build up credibility in the debt market before drawing down on that credibility by borrowing to the maximum extent and then ultimately defaulting on the debt, either directly or by inflating away the value of the debt.[32] This is the Latin American pattern, and it appears to be the future pattern of the United States.[33]

Is such a future avoidable? Yes, but avoidance of the pattern is unlikely. We probably have a limited amount of time left to start making adjustments. There are a few vicious cycles that endanger our longevity if imbalances persist for another five years or so.

The first involves budget deficits. The federal debt is the cumulative result of our past budget account deficits. If the federal debt continues to grow more rapidly than GDP, the potential increase in debt service as a proportion of the budget could make getting the deficit under control nearly impossible. Furthermore, as our debt-to-GDP ratio becomes large, increases in Treasury bond interest rates tend to be self-reinforcing in the absence of aggressive Federal Reserve intervention. Any increase in interest rates on Treasury bonds implies a larger percentage of the budget going to

---

[32] Carmen M. Reinhart and Kenneth S. Rogoff, This Time Is Different: Eight Centuries of Financial Folly (Princeton, NJ: Princeton University Press, 2009).

[33] Paul Blustein's two books, And the Money Kept Rolling In (and Out): Wall Street, the IMF, and the Bankrupting of Argentina (New York: Public Affairs, 2005) and The Chastening: Inside the Crisis that Rocked the Global Financial System and Humbled the IMF (New York: Public Affairs, 2003), are excellent resources for the reader to explore the similarities of Latin American macroeconomic patterns with those of the United States.

interest payments on the federal debt, which in turn implies more future budget weakness and further interest rate increases.

The second vicious cycle endangering the United States involves our current account deficit. Since World War II, our current account has gone through three distinct phases. In the first phase, lasting from 1945 to 1965, we sold more goods and services to the rest of the world than the rest of the world sold to us, and as a result we increased our ownership position in overseas assets. Our trading partners paid for the trade deficits they ran by giving us ownership interests in their assets. The second phase, lasting from 1965 to 1995, was an interregnum period during which the Unites States ran current account deficits but continued to have a hugely net positive balance in international assets. It was during the third phase, lasting from 1995 to the present, that vicious cycles begin to kick in; since 1990, our net international investment position has been negative, and we have continued to run large current account deficits.

If our net international investment position becomes sufficiently negative, then the current account deficit can become difficult or impossible to reverse, because a large transfer is required simply to pay the return on US assets held by foreigners. This is a fact of international trade that is not widely understood. Once you become a debtor nation, your current account deficit is roughly equal to the trade deficit (the deficit in trade of goods and services) plus the net return that you have to pay the international investors who own your assets. When you become sufficiently dug in, it becomes nearly impossible to recover, because your trade balance must experience massive growth just to bring your current account balance to zero.

Most countries throughout history haven't had the two great luxuries that the United States has: they haven't been able to print their own currency in unlimited supply, and they haven't been able to borrow exclusively in their home currency. If you can't print money, or you can print money but you have to borrow in another currency whose printing you don't control, then the vicious cycles described above go to work in quick and severe fashion. It can be "game over" for a currency pretty quickly, in the sense that your currency's relative value can bottom out. When you can print money and borrow in the same currency, the situation is both better and infinitely more complicated. It's better not because it solves any of the fundamental problems but rather because it gives you more degrees of freedom in solving those fundamental problems over time.

***

The reason that harsh budget austerity (bringing the budget all the way into balance next year, let's just say) represents certain political disaster is simple: asset prices of all kinds would go a long way toward zero, and the poor and much of the middle class would have no assets and little or no income. Debt levels in all sectors of the American economy—individual, business, and government—are extremely high. If the federal government sharply contracts its spending, it would likely lead to a vicious cycle of debt-deflation in both stocks and real estate, where initial declines in asset values lead to forced liquidations (due to high debt levels), which in turn lead to further declines in assets values and further forced liquidations. It is only extraordinary levels of government spending that prevented this process from proceeding a very long way in the fall of 2008.

The exact form that political disaster might take is anyone's guess. It could emerge from immensely misguided policy on the part of ignorant politicians. It could result in riots in major cities. It could mean a rapid uptick in crime and civil disruption. It could even take the form of a slow death, where people quit paying taxes and abdicate civic responsibility, as in Greece. The main reason that budget austerity would lead to political disruption is that, implicitly, a tenuous bargain has been struck in US society. Although income and wealth inequality are very high, the highest in the developed world, our collective bargain states that the social fabric will remain vaguely intact as long as high government spending provides some minimal level of support. Without government programs, large swathes of our economic society would be fully decimated.

We can expect to see an aggressive continuation of the debt monetization that started in March 18, 2009, when the Federal Reserve announced that it would be buying $300 billion in US Treasuries in the open market. Faced with difficulties in finding foreign lenders, the US Treasury will come to expect the Federal Reserve to buy US Treasury bonds on the open market on an ongoing basis. This feeds into the vicious cycles mentioned above, as such debt monetization fuels expectations of future inflation, pushing long-term interest rates higher.

Our predicament, roughly, is this: because the government issues dollars and has dollar-denominated debt, we can always choose to push our problems further into the future at the risk of increased future inflation. Lately, we've been choosing that policy option quite a lot, leading many observers to anticipate dramatically high inflation at some point in the future. A recent example of the trend's continuation is so-called QE4, the Federal Reserve's September 2012 announcement of its intention to purchase $40 billion in mortgage-backed securities and other assets "until such improvement is achieved in a context of price stability." When a country buys back its own assets with its own dollars, it's merely printing money.

My view on both the current account deficit and the budget deficit is somewhat of a paradox. Historically, I've been inclined toward economic orthodoxy—our best policy option is to continue to run high budget and current account deficits, even though these deficits will push us right up against the brink of disaster. That is: when choosing between uncertain disaster and certain disaster, chose uncertain disaster. My belief is that politics trumps economics; you only get in real trouble as a country when people fail to get along. There's a risk that high current account deficits, high inflation, and high debt-to-GDP ratios will translate into political problems far down the road, but I think it's a near certainty that the type of budget austerity envisioned by Tea Party candidates and disastrously enacted in Europe would bring immediate political problems.

2 FIAT CURRENCY AND THE TEMPTATIONS OF SEIGNIORAGE

One of the first lessons in finance is that if your estimate differs from the consensus view that is embedded in market prices, then most likely you are in error—not the market. The cognitive dissonance inherent in our economic environment is this: we will see fairly high rates of inflation in the future, yet the yield on thirty-year US Treasuries at the time of this writing is 3.05 percent, implying a very low rate of expected inflation.[35]

Deflation and hyperinflation are often seen as being exclusive and opposite states. This seems logical, since the former involves a decrease in

---

[35] US Department of the Treasury, Daily Treasury Yield Curve, January 2013, http://www.treasury.gov/resource-center/data-chart-center/interest-rates/Pages/TextView.aspx?data=yield (accessed January 11, 2013).

the price level and the latter involves a rapid increase. But the two conditions are actually quite close to one another, and, when an economy enters a period of crisis, it's something of a razor's-edge phenomenon whether the economy experiences deflation or high inflation. On one side, people hoard cash and cash equivalents and feel comfortable trading in cash and cash equivalents instead of assets; this is the deflationary scenario. On the other side, people are nervous about the currency as a store of wealth (they don't trust government policy and they don't trust any nonmaterial good or non-asset store of wealth); this is the inflationary scenario.

A country cannot easily flip from high inflation to deflation but may flip from deflation to high inflation through monetary policy—through printing huge amounts of money, for instance. The likelihood of the inflationary case in general depends on people's confidence in the government, and on the extent of money supply growth that has occurred in the past and is expected to occur in the future. To give an example, few individuals in the United States and abroad would be willing to invest in Treasuries if the Fed just printed trillions of dollars and a can of soda now cost $5 instead of 50¢. An investor would think to himself, "What if this happens again, and my investment is instantly worth a fraction of its value?" Investment products aside, simply holding US dollars would be undesirable in this scenario, as the dollar's ability to buy goods or assets of any kind would be in free-fall. Let's look more in-depth.

Over the long run, inflation is primarily a function of money supply growth; a doubling of the money supply will ultimately cause something approximating a doubling of the price level. Over the short and medium term, inflation is a function of money supply growth and monetary velocity. Monetary velocity is essentially the speed at which a currency unit travels through the economy. When people are hoarding, velocity is very low;

when the economy is running strong, velocity tends to be high. The hyperinflationary dynamic is primarily about monetary velocity.

In my view, there are four basic causes of very high rates of inflation. The first, and easiest to understand, is a complete lack of confidence in the survival of the backer of the currency unit. If a government looks like it might collapse, and the collapse of the government brings with it a loss in the value of the currency, then the price of goods will go up rapidly in terms of the currency unit. The inflation rate of the Confederate States of America, always high due to excessive monetary growth,[36] went parabolic toward the end of the Civil War as it became clear that the Confederacy would lose.[37]

The second cause of inflation is egregious money supply growth by the central authorities. The classic example is Weimar Germany: the German government printed massive amounts of currency to pay off heavy war reparations dictated by the Treaty of Versailles. At the Versailles Conference, John Maynard Keynes argued for a more generous peace. After his advice went unheeded, he penned *The Economic Consequences of the Peace*, wherein he predicted subsequent German hyperinflation. German inflation reached monthly rates of 10,000 percent in 1923. By late 1923, the Weimar government had issued a one-hundred-trillion-mark banknote.[38]

The most stunning recent example of money supply growth–driven inflation occurred in Zimbabwe. The head of the Reserve Bank of

---

[36] Douglas B. Ball, Financial Failure and the Confederate Defeat (Urbana: University of Illinois Press, 1991).

[37] Marc Weidenmier, "Money and Finance in the Confederate States of America," http://eh.net/encyclopedia/article/weidenmier.finance.confederacy.us (accessed November 1, 2011);

Eugene M. Lerner, "Money, Prices and Wages in the Confederacy, 1861–1865," Journal of Political Economy 63, no. 1 (1955): 20–40.

[38] Eric D. Weitz, Weimar Germany: Promise and Tragedy (Princeton, NJ: Princeton University Press, 2007), 135.

Zimbabwe, Gideon Gono, said in a January 2009 *Newsweek* interview, "I've been condemned by traditional economists who said that printing money is responsible for inflation. Out of the necessity to exist, to ensure my people survive, I had to find myself printing money."[39] In early 2007, Zimbabwe was experiencing a monthly inflation rate of 13.7 percent. It skyrocketed to annualized rates of 41,200,000 percent by June of 2008 and a mind-boggling 89.7 sextillion percent (89,700,000,000,000,000,000,000 percent) by November of that year.[40] From January to December 2008, the money supply growth rose from 81,143 percent to 658 billion percent.[41] Such is the power of an irresponsible central bank. In an interesting coincidence, the Central Bank of Zimbabwe also issued a one-hundred-trillion-dollar banknote at the peak of its desperation.[42]

The third case is a collapse in the value of the exchange rate. This occurs when a country cannot modify its import demand—when it imports things deemed necessary, such as food. Iceland provides a recent example of this concept. A collapse in the Icelandic krona caused a nearly immediate rapid rise in prices.[43] Iceland, further, had an extremely high ratio of external debt-to-exports.[44] Analysts of the American predicament often underestimate the importance of this metric. Iceland, unfortunately, had

---

[39] Newsweek, "It Can't Be Any Worse," Interview with Gideon Gono, January 24, 2009, http://www.newsweek.com/id/181221 (accessed November 3, 2011).
[40] Steven H. Hanke, "R.I.P. Zimbabwe Dollar," CATO Institute, http://www.cato.org/zimbabwe (accessed November 3, 2011).
[41] Financial Gazette (Zimbabwe), "When a Lot of Money Is Bad," February 6, 2009, http://www.financialgazette.co.zw/?option=com_content&view=article&id=351:when-a-lot-of-money-is-bad&catid=32:companies-a-markets&Itemid=47 (accessed November 3, 2011).
[42] The Herald, "RBZ Unveils $100 Trillion Dollar Note," January 16, 2009, http://www.herald.co.zw/inside.aspx?sectid=153&cat=1 (accessed January 13, 2013).

[43] For detailed statistics, see Statistics Iceland, http://www.statice.is/Statistics (accessed November 3, 2011).

[44] Ibid. See also Jeremy Batstone, "Is Iceland Facing a Meltdown?," Money Week, May 18, 2006, http://www.moneyweek.com/news-and-charts/economics/is-iceland-facing-a-meltdown (accessed November 3, 2011).

most of its debt denominated in foreign currencies such as the euro. This meant that, in crisis, the real value of its debt burden increased hugely, as a single krona became worth a smaller and smaller portion of every other currency. Iceland provides little to the world economy (fish, mostly) relative to what it likes to take. The country seemed in danger, in 2009, of having its people lose faith in its currency and government. A lack of faith can, in itself, put inflationary pressure on modern fiat currencies; as George Soros points out, equilibrium in markets is not the norm—the norm involves virtuous and vicious cycles and far-from-equilibrium paths.[45] Fortunately, by 2013, Iceland had made a substantial recovery, aided in no small way by rowdy groups of jet-setting bankers from New York and London, flush with newly printed Bank of England and Federal Reserve money, and eager to take on Reykjavík.

The fourth case is the most interesting, as the underlying problem is too much money supply growth, but the direct push toward hyperinflation is an increase in monetary velocity. Typically, the start to this process is a severe economic downturn. In a downturn, monetary velocity tends to slow significantly. Monetary velocity is depressed, economic activity is depressed, and, quite probably, money supply has seen a temporary downtick as a result of private credit destruction. There is a reflexive political urge to do something; that something typically involves both fiscal and monetary stimulus.

The monetary authorities are often misled by the low level of monetary velocity that they see during recessions. Specifically, if they are targeting price level rather than money supply growth, there is the danger that after

---

[45] George Soros, The Alchemy of Finance: Reading the Mind of the Market (New York: John Wiley & Sons, 1994).

growing the money supply and observing no response in the price level, they will be encouraged to grow the money supply a bit more. Arguably we are seeing this now in the United States. It's likely that Federal Reserve chairman Ben Bernanke is overconfident in his ability to withdraw liquidity as necessary when the economy heats up. Alas, just as Keynesian economics tends to be distorted such that we run big deficits in good times and really big deficits in bad times, monetary economics has tended to be distorted such that we inject credit in bad times but don't withdraw it in good times.

If the monetary authorities are unable or unwilling to withdraw liquidity from the system as the economy normalizes, then the full impact of the monetary creation that was undertaken during the crisis period will become apparent when economic activity and monetary velocity normalize. Often this monetary creation is sizable, and thus the resultant inflation is quite high. If inflation is high enough, the economy enters a negative feedback loop whereby high inflation increases monetary velocity. This increased monetary velocity increases the inflation rate, which increases monetary velocity further, ad infinitum. When inflation is 20 percent per year, you will show a weak preference for buying today rather than buying tomorrow. When inflation is 20 percent per week, you will seldom purchase tomorrow what you can purchase today. When inflation is 20 percent per day, you will make purchases as soon as the need arises. When inflation is extremely high, money becomes something to get rid of in favor of goods as quickly as possible.

The dynamic interaction between monetary velocity and inflation is the primary reason inflation rate targeting doesn't work. There are times when a government would like to be able to inflate in a controlled way. Now is such a time in the United States. A large percentage of American households and business have negative worth at the moment.[46] A deflationary environment would cause the debts of these groups to grow in real terms. There's a danger that a decent slice of the population could feel crushed by their debts and become disenchanted with the system. Inflation, on the other hand, would allow the real burdens of these debts to slowly ease. Let's not forget that inflation would also lower the debt burden of the US government; particularly beneficial, as a bit over half the debt is held by foreigners.[47] Controlled inflation should create short-term increases in consumption and investment demand. Nonetheless, the evidence suggests that it's difficult to stage controlled inflation, especially if you are talking about more than 4 percent or 5 percent per year.

A core issue is that no one has any idea at all what the money supply is. The complications are such that the most educated observers can hardly begin to think about how one should define or measure the money supply. As recently as the mid-1990s, people used to talk about various measures of the money supply as if they meant something. Now, private credit creation swamps public credit creation, and no one has figured out quite how to think about the problem systematically. Essentially, it's very hard to place a dollar value on a faith-based credit contract when the currency itself is faith-based.

As Peter Warburton notes, in *Debt and Delusion*, "[T]he issue of bonds by governments and companies, business and trade credit, financial market credit (e.g., sale and repurchase facilities, stock lending) and derivative

---

[46] US Federal Reserve, Balance Sheet of Households and Non-Profit Organizations, http://www.federalreserve.gov/releases/Z1/current/z1r-5.pdf (accessed November 3, 2011).

[47] US Treasury, Major Foreign Holders of Treasury Securities, http://www.treas.gov/tic/mfh.txt (accessed November 3, 2011); for debt broken down by type, see US Treasury, Preliminary Report on Foreign Holdings of US Securities, http://www.treas.gov/tic/shlprelim.html (accessed August 10, 2009).

market credit are all examples of activities through which additional purchasing power can be released into the economy or the asset markets."[48]

In macroeconomics textbooks, there used to be graphs of money velocity over time. A calculation of, say, GDP divided by M2 (a fairly broad measure of the money supply used by the Federal Reserve) was used to calculate monetary velocity. That might or might not have been a meaningful exercise then. Today, it is definitely meaningless. So, if you have no idea what the money supply is, then you really have no idea what money velocity is—you can only say, vaguely, that it is much lower now than it was a few years ago. I don't see how inflation rate targeting can possibly work in an environment of unstable monetary velocity and an immeasurable money supply. This is not to mention the fact that the unconventional liquidity policies that we've seen in recent years have made the lags associated with monetary policy more uncertain than ever before.

When an economy enters severe stress, cash flow rather than net worth becomes the most important factor for individuals and businesses. As Michael Lewis said of Iceland, "[A] society that has been ruined overnight doesn't look much different from how it did the day before, when it believed itself to be richer than ever."[49] Wealth changes don't affect behavior much on a day-to-day basis; cash flow does. Serious economic and political unrest doesn't start until large segments of the economy run out of cash.

***

---

[48] Peter Warburton, Debt and Delusion (London: Allen Lane/Penguin, 1999), 45.

[49] Michael Lewis, "Wall Street on the Tundra," Vanity Fair, April 2009, http://www.vanityfair.com/politics/features/2009/04/iceland200904 (accessed November 3, 2011).

The subject of job creation and destruction is treacherous territory. Assertions frequently run counter to economic logic; particularly problematic is the suggestion that the economy will run out of jobs. New jobs find a way to create themselves. One need only look at Los Angeles or New York to see which unlikely new industry will spring up to employ people—the latest seems to be the move toward personal chefs.

Those who suggest that new technologies will leave a large segment of people jobless are simply bound to be wrong in the long term; as technology allows more work to be done by fewer people, workers made redundant will find employment in some new area. The wealth creation that occurs as a result of improved productivity allows a society to create industries and jobs that service more specialized consumer needs.

It's possible that technology, global wage competition, and financial crisis are creating what is potentially a medium-term (five- to ten-year) job shortage in the United States. A job shortage might lead to a cash shortage among consumers that is unprecedented in the modern era. If this transpires, it will make the monetary policy environment extremely challenging, and it will make the political environment somewhat explosive.

Government action during this crisis has perhaps relied too heavily on monetary policy as opposed to measures that get cash directly into people's hands, especially those people who need it most it and are most inclined to spend it. One problem with monetary measures in a deep crisis is that those who are close to the monetary spigot benefit disproportionately. Since credit creation mostly occurs through the banking system, we find that those who benefit from monetary stimulus are, above all, the bankers, followed closely by those who owe the bankers money. Further down the line, the shop owner in New York City or Charlotte benefits much more than someone in a small midwestern town.

Cash levels are essential to understanding the inflationary dynamic. To the average consumer, one particularly maddening set of circumstances is inflation coupled with low cash level. In rich countries, where credit is widely available, the worst-off often have a negative net worth. Inflation lowers the real value of their debt, and so one might think it's welcome. In fact, however, people's dominant consideration is the fact that their cash flows are depleting. In Argentina, say, during the 2001–2002 crisis, even for those who had negative net worth (such that hyperinflation was improving their wealth scenario), inflation was eating away what little cash they had left.[50] Recall Gideon Gono's statement regarding Zimbabwean hyperinflation: when high inflation gets in, the poor run out of money and encourage politicians to print more of it.

I'm often stunned by analysts who suggest that the deflationary forces following the economic crisis that started in late summer 2007 are potentially too strong for the Federal Reserve to counter. Let us get one thing straight: if the Federal Reserve has a desire to create inflation, they will succeed. Ben Bernanke clarified matters in a November 21, 2002, speech:

> Like gold, US dollars have value only to the extent that they are strictly limited in supply. But the US government has a technology, called a printing press (or, today, its electronic equivalent), that allows it to produce as many US dollars as it wishes at essentially no cost. By increasing the number of US dollars in circulation, or even by credibly threatening to do so, the US government can also reduce the value of a dollar in terms of goods and services, which is equivalent to raising the prices in dollars of those goods and services.[51]

---

[50] Blustein, And the Money Kept Rolling In (And Out).

[51] Ben Bernanke, "Deflation: Making Sure 'It' Doesn't Happen Here": Remarks by Governor Ben Bernanke Before the National Economists Club, November 21, 2002,

In response to the recent crisis, the Fed has unleashed a stunning arsenal of liquidity creation tools. On March 18, 2009, the Federal Reserve announced that it would begin buying $300 billion in long-term Treasury bonds. This became widely known as QE (quantitative easing); it was followed up by QE2 in 2010, and QE3 and QE4 in 2012. The policy of buying long-term government bonds on the open market amounts to a direct monetization of the federal debt that will lead to high inflation and currency debasement if continued.

The policy arguments for monetizing the long-term debt rest on very shaky intellectual foundations. In a reasonably efficient financial market, the price of a security is a function of the underlying economic reality. Price should only change when the economic reality is changing. The price of Microsoft stock will change drastically if it announces some material change to its business reality; if a mutual fund manager at Fidelity sells one million shares for liquidity reasons, you will hardly see a blip in price. The market will accommodate the manager's liquidity demand at something close to what it deems to be the proper long-term price for Microsoft stock. Although this sounds overly abstract, empirical finance research suggests that markets work in approximately this way.[52] Why, then, would government purchases substantially affect yields on long-term Treasury bonds over any but the shortest time horizons? If anything, these Treasury bond purchases should cause rates to go up over the medium and long term, as investors revise their estimates of expected future inflation upward.

A disturbing prospect is that we might one day reach a point in the United States where continued monetization of the debt is the only way we

---

http://www.federalreserve.gov/BOARDDOCS/SPEECHES/2002/20021121/default.htm (accessed November 2011, 2011).

[52] For a more thorough discussion, see Andrei Shleifer, "Do Demand Curves for Stocks Slope Down?," Journal of Finance 41, no. 3 (July 1996).

can fund government operations. I don't see this coming any time soon, but we are on the path. When the Treasury is not able to fund its current expenditures with tax inflows (all the time, in other words), it raises money by selling bonds at auction. If one of those auctions were to fail, the Treasury would not be able to fund government operations, and government activity would slowly grind to a halt. An equivalent scenario played out in 2001 in Argentina; the country couldn't sell its bonds in auctions, and government activity would have ground to a halt without IMF assistance.

Markets assign a nonzero probability to a US government default. This is because the United States might find it in its best interest to default at some point in the distant future and because there is the theoretical possibility that the Chairman of the Federal Reserve at the time of failing Treasury auctions will be a recalcitrant inflation hawk who refuses to create money for the purpose of buying Treasury debt. The Treasury is supposed to be constrained in this way; some suggest that there are legal loopholes that allow Treasury to circumvent the constraint. Consider the late 2012/early 2013 discussions of the "trillion dollar coin."[53]

In my view, the problem with creating inflation as a matter of policy in the current environment is that you will harm those hardest hit by the crisis, at least in the short term. A policy of inflation is effective at stimulating activity because it improves the balance sheets of indebted consumers and businesses, and because it encourages economic actors to consume and invest sooner rather than later. In other words, the prospect of future inflation gets people who already have money to spend it now, before prices go up. This harms people who have little in the way of cash balances—it causes their cash to run out more quickly. There are reasons to

---

[53] Stephen L. Carter, "The Platinum Coin: It's a Really Bad Idea," Bloomberg News, January 10, 2013, http://www.bloomberg.com/news/2013-01-10/the-platinum-coin-it-s-a-really-bad-idea.html.

believe that there will be many people in the current crisis who are forced into situations where they need to get by on small cash balances. In the absence of substantial income replacement and income assistance programs over a long period of time, fairly high rates of inflation will become politically untenable.

Our monetary policy instruments are somewhat crude. There is no way, through monetary policy, to get cash or credit into the hands of people who really need them. In the recent era, bubbles have been the natural outgrowth of money supply growth. We have little ability to redirect new credit money, so we end up with some self-reinforcing mess of investment in unproductive assets (most recently, overinvestment in Internet business, telecommunications, and real estate).

To a greater degree than is generally assumed, inflation is driven by human psychology. The history of Weimar Germany suggests that inflation can take people by surprise; to the man on the street, the move from normality to hyperinflation occurred very quickly. Hyperinflation is as much a function of confidence in the system as it is in the printing press. In the current US situation, the money for massive inflation already exists—it's just very comfortable sitting in paper form and in financial assts. If the rate at which Americans choose to convert assets into real goods and services (or, more likely, the commodities that are used in the production of goods and services) speeds up, then inflation will result.

One of the most amazing aspects of our long boom was that money was so comfortable going into financial assets. It is this phenomenon that Robert Shiller had in mind when he described "moral anchors" to financial bubbles in his book *Irrational Exuberance*. The simplest explanation for a financial bubble is that a speculation-driven economy is like musical chairs, where continuance of the system requires that no one is checking on how many seats are available. In 1999, the claims on wealth had increased by over 100 percent in three years. Clearly, actual wealth hadn't gone up nearly as fast. The claims on wealth were likely already overvalued at the time of Alan Greenspan's "irrational exuberance" speech. Continuation of the bubble requires that no one try to "cash in" paper wealth—if too many people try to cash in, they will quickly find that there is not enough real wealth to back up the claims on wealth.

Economists describe a financial market as allocationally efficient if capital tends to flow to projects where it can be used most efficiently. Inflation impairs the ability of a market to be allocationally efficient, because one adds an additional layer of complexity on top of the already difficult task of assessing project risk and project cash flows. For the purposes of investment decisions, inflation is not too big of a problem if it is steady and predictable. When it is uncertain and potentially high, as now, it wreaks havoc on investment decisions.

Taxes are based on nominal capital gains and nominal income, so in a regime of high expected inflation, the expected real tax rate can be quite high. An investor is taxed not only on the return on capital but also on a piece of the return of capital. If tax rates go up over the next few years, and inflationary expectations kick up, we can expect a low level of investment. Particularly hard hit are areas of investment where the probability of loss is high.

At the moment, there are still a fair number of people who believe that we might be locked into a long-term deflationary cycle, where the inflation rate will remain very low or even negative for five to ten years. Proponents of this view point to the massive destruction in private credit, the difficulty of reigniting credit growth in a world with few creditworthy projects or borrowers, and the near impossibility of price increases in the face of record worldwide excess capacity. Indeed, Japan's experience in the 1990s was one of stubbornly low or negative inflation, despite a fairly strong political will to create inflation.[54] I believe that the political will within the United States for an avoidance of deflation is simply too strong for deflation or even very low inflation to be the US reality over the next ten years. My outlook is for low to negative inflation over the next two to four years, followed by fairly high to potentially very high inflation for at least the subsequent fifteen years.

I think by far the most likely scenario is that we will experience high rates of inflation, with a perhaps 30 percent chance of sustained inflation rates of over 15 percent per year at some point over the next fifteen years. It's almost impossible to tell when high inflation rates might come. There's some shot, perhaps 10 percent, that high inflation will come early—in the next four years, say. The most likely scenario for early inflation would be a very sharp decline in the dollar.

If the Federal Reserve continues to engage in extensive debt monetization, as I think likely, then high inflation rates in the future are a near guarantee. Debt monetization amounts to an expansion of the money supply and is directly inflationary. Further, as a central bank monetizes its government's debt, it loses its political independence. This is debatable in the case of the Federal Reserve, but it's a historical regularity, and, to me, a loss of independence at the Federal Reserve has been strongly evident in the past five years. We can reasonably doubt whether a Federal Reserve that has extensively monetized debt would be willing to raise interest rates as inflationary pressures become evident, when the effect of an interest rate increase would be to directly increase the debt service costs of an already strained federal government.

---

[54] A detailed economic analysis of the Japanese predicament can be found in Richard Werner's brilliant book New Paradigm in Macroeconomics: Solving the Riddle of Japanese Macroeconomic Performance (Houndmills, Basingstoke, Hampshire, and New York: Palgrave Macmillan, 2005).

A likely scenario is that the much bemoaned asymmetry in fiscal and monetary policy will emerge in a new guise. The Federal Reserve will use times of weakness as an excuse to engage in debt monetization. The stated reason for this monetization will be to stimulate the economy by lowering long-term interest rates. Economic logic suggests that it's impossible to lower long-term interest rates through Federal Reserve purchases of long-date Treasuries for any but the shortest time periods, but lowering long-term interest rates will nevertheless be the stated purpose of the Federal Reserve, as it was during the March 2009 announcement of debt monetization.

The best barometers of inflation for individuals to pay attention to are commodity prices, especially gold and oil. Keep in mind, though, that commodity prices are on a long-run secular upward trend driven by the integration of China and India into the world economy, and the inexorable mathematics of exponential population and economic growth against a backdrop of scarce resources.[55] There is every reason to believe that governments will act to deter speculators in commodity markets, especially markets such as gold or silver that are thought to provide a strong signal of expected future inflation. We can expect occasional interventions in these markets where the objective is abrupt downward price changes.

We're becoming deeply addicted to debt monetization, with likely dire consequences. There's a bizarre aspect of debt monetization in the United States that tends to feed the addiction. The balance sheet of the Federal Reserve consists primarily of US government debt and US government guaranteed agency debt. The Fed earns interest on these holdings of debt.

---

[55] Don Stammber, "Resource Prices on a Long-Term Uptrend," The Australian, August 14, 2012, http://bit.ly/WqPr83 (accessed January 27, 2013). Also see Jeremy Grantham's April 2011 Quarterly Letter for GMO: "Time to Wake Up: Days of Abundant Resources and Falling Prices Are Over Forever," http://www.energybulletin.net/stories/2011-04-29/time-wake-days-abundant-resources-and-falling-prices-are-over-forever (accessed February 7, 2013).

Any profit earned by the Federal Reserve is turned over to the Treasury. In 2012, the Federal Reserve turned over $89 billion in "profits" to the Treasury.[56] This strange mechanism implies that the Treasury is able to borrow from the Fed interest-free.

Of the $89 billion remitted to Treasury from the Fed, $13.3 billion came from gains on Treasuries it sold. This is sobering: what do we suppose happens if the Fed announces that it will cut down on its buying of Treasuries? The Treasury yield will go up, and the Treasury will get hit twice; first because it will now have to pay market rates on its new debt (instead of the zero percent effective interest it pays when the Fed buys the debt), and second because the increase in rates will cause the Fed to suffer a capital loss on the bonds it sells from its portfolio, and this loss is ultimately borne by Treasury.

We can safely predict that the longer the period of weakness and low inflation extends from 2013, the more severe inflation will be when it arrives. A long period of weakness will encourage extensive debt monetization. When recovery finally arrives, the Federal Reserve will be hesitant to rein in previous liquidity creation and thereby raise rates, because, as noted, this would serve to increase the financial difficulties of the government. I will go as far as to predict that, even when recovery arrives, the Federal Reserve will be hesitant to slow down the rate of new debt monetization, as the Treasury will have come to rely on it. This suggests that any sustained economic strength, when it comes, will be strongly inflationary, as it will bring to light the effects of past monetary creation. Economic strength, though, is not a necessary condition for high inflation; a severe drop in the dollar and/or a strong run-up in commodity

---

[56] Kristina Peterson, "$88.9 Billion: Fed Payout to Treasury," Wall Street Journal, January 10, 2012, http://online.wsj.com/article/SB10001424127887324081704578233592472455634.html.

prices are an expected result of money creation and can bring about high inflation in the absence of economic strength.

3 A STRANGE SYMBIOSIS

China is no longer the shaky newcomer. Although their GDP per capita is still unimpressive ($8,400, compared with $48,300 in the United States, a mere 17.4 percent), the world is giving them some credit for expected future performance.[57] Their population is by far the biggest of any nation on earth (1.34 billion); this, combined with their high national savings rate of 38 percent, has quickly turned them into one of the world's biggest creditor nations despite their low income.[58]

---

[57] Central Intelligence Agency, The World Factbook. "Economy, Overview," https://www.cia.gov/library/publications/the-world-factbook/geos/us.html (accessed January 12, 2013).

[58] "Getting Chinese to Stop Savings and Start Spending Is a Hard Sell," Washington Post, July 5, 2012.

China had fifteen cities with over five million people as of April 2011.[59] The growth rates of these cities have been staggering. The United States has nine cities with over 1 million people; China has over fifty.[60] Most of the population is engaged in manufacturing. Sixteen of the twenty most polluted cities in the world are in China.[61] Experts say that the world's shortage of treated water will be felt severely in China in upcoming decades. China's Yellow River, the fourth longest in the world, is so overexploited that it failed to reach its endpoint, the East China Sea, in eighteen of the last twenty-five years of the twentieth century. In one year, 1997, it failed to reach the sea for 226 days.[62] Although the average manufacturing wage in China has climbed to $2.50 an hour including (highly limited) benefits, from about 60 cents in 2000, workers typically remit a large portion of their pay to their extended families.[63]

On my visits to China, I have been struck by the following thought: I have produced no tangible products of any value and few intangible products, and yet I live very high; the Chinese produce things that are of

---

[59] "Communiqué of the National Bureau of Statistics of People's Republic of China on Major Figures of the 2010 Population Census[1]" (No.2) National Bureau of Statistics Of China," http://www.stats.gov.cn/english/newsandcomingevents/t20110429_402722516.htm (accessed January 12, 2013).

[60] US Census Bureau, Metropolitan and Micropolitan Statistical Areas, "Annual Estimates of the Population of Metropolitan and Micropolitan Statistical Areas," July 1, 2011, Census; "Communiqué," NBSC, 2010.

[61] Grant Halloway, "Invisible Enemy Spurs Health Worries," CNN. June 2, 2006, http://www.cnn.com/2006/HEALTH/conditions/05/09/air.pollution/index.html (accessed November 2011).

[62] Rob Gifford, China Road: A Journey into the Future of a Rising Power (New York: Random House, 2007), 135–36.

[63] David Luhnow, "For Mexico, an Edge on China," Wall Street Journal, September 16, 2012, http://professional.wsj.com/article/SB10000872396390444318104577587191288101170.html?mg=reno64-wsj (accessed January 27, 2013).

obvious value to the world and yet live close to the bone. I had to go to China to realize the obvious: the big twenty- or thirty-year trend in my life will be relative improvement in living standards in China and other disciplined developing countries and a relative decline in living standards in the United States.

But it is not merely enough for China to maintain its growth rate. The growth has to be of the right type. Specifically, it should be export-oriented growth, to provide for continuing growth in the manufacturing sector in major cities.

In the midst of the financial crisis, the Chinese government launched an ambitious spending program to take up the slack from a decline in manufacturing unemployment, and thus far the program appears to have been successful. Indeed, Chinese government policy in the past twenty-five years has been to accumulate large foreign reserves, while encouraging high national savings—in effect, creating the biggest rainy day fund in the history of international economics. So far, this rainy day fund appears to have successfully ensured high GDP growth. We will not know for a while whether simply maintaining high GDP growth is enough to keep the Chinese happy; it might be necessary to have export-oriented manufacturing growth. This type of growth doesn't appear likely over the next few years, given the economic constraints of China's major customers, the United States and Europe.

One of the problems with government spending growth is this: though by all accounts the manufacturing business in China is a brutal enterprise, a sort of man-eat-man world, the Chinese seem to understand and even appreciate the rules, and the choices made over the past twenty-five years suggest that growth in manufacturing employment has represented a large positive change in people's lives. By contrast, direct government spending programs will always be seen by the Chinese as corrupt and unfair, and will tend to increase discontent with the political system.

China has a national savings rate of nearly 54 percent.[64] Martin Wolf, in *Fixing Global Finance*, observes that this might be the highest national savings rate of any country ever in modern history.[65] The only other country to reach this level is the tiny kingdom of Bhutan.[66] A national savings rate as high as China's is hard to square with economic rationality for a country growing as quickly as China; it is the equivalent of an individual penny-pinching in his twenties so as to increase savings, when he is nearly guaranteed high income in his thirties and forties. It's not in doubt that the high saver will be richer in later years; it's just thought that the utility gained by spending the money earlier exceeds the utility loss associated with being somewhat less rich in later years. As noted, the government's motive for promoting a high savings rate appears to be the establishment of a large contingency fund. Unlike Western countries, in China, much of the savings, directly or indirectly, remains in the control of the government. In establishing a large contingency fund, the Chinese government is learning from countless previous examples of developing countries without such a fund; after one or two missteps, such countries can become pariahs of the international economy and fall off their growth path for ten years or more.

---

[64] Yin Zhang and Guanghua Wan, National Savings and Balanced Growth: China vs. India, World Bank Presentation, http://siteresources.worldbank.org/INTDECABCTOK2006/Resources/Yin_Zhang&Guanghua_Wan.ppt (accessed November 3, 2011); International Monetary Fund, "Gross National Savings Rate (% of GDP)," updated August 2011. Viewable via http://www.economywatch.com/economic-statistics/economic-indicators/Gross_National_Savings_Percentage_of_GDP/ (accessed January 27, 2013).

[65] Martin Wolf, Fixing Global Finance, Forum on Constructive Capitalism (Baltimore: Johns Hopkins University Press, February 2010).

The Chinese government's encouragement of a high savings rate comes more from negative incentives than positive ones. Western governments shy away from fear as a motivator; China does not. At the individual level, much of the high savings rate can be explained by a lack of social safety nets and by the lack of a health care system. If China wanted to lower its savings rate at some point as a matter of policy, the implementation of some basic social safety net provisions would be the best long-term solution. The lack of health care creates a strong culture among families to save, because it's clear that if one extended family member becomes sick, the presence or absence of savings can make the difference between life and death.

China's human rights record and its failure to provide income or health care support is not just a moral issue; it's a political stability issue. How long will people in a rich country stand being treated badly? China's political system is not consistent with freedom and wealth accumulation. That is not the end of the world. Every political system is flawed. Depending on whom you speak with, capitalist democracies are flawed because the majority can vote themselves wealth or because the rich establish a monopoly on access to those in power. To the extent that China runs into internal political problems, I suspect that they will play out over a fairly long horizon (ten to forty years). Nonetheless, there will always be an internal inconsistency in the strategy of economic liberalization without political liberation that was launched by Deng Xiaoping. When people become rich, they typically make it plain that they no longer want anyone telling them what to do.

In the early 1980s, as the Soviet Union was pursuing political reform in the absence of economic reform, China under Deng was pursuing a fairly rapid move toward market economics and global trade without any moves toward political reform. Agitation for political reform manifested itself in the Tiananmen Square protests of 1989. The military crackdown in

Tiananmen Square, in which approximately 2,500 people were killed and 7,000–10,000 were injured,[67] showed a remarkable disregard for international opinion, as the protests leading up to the crackdown were extensively covered by international media. The crackdown starkly showed the Western world that no matter how far China had come in economic reforms, it was a long way from relaxing centralized political control, and it showed the Chinese people themselves that protests were to some extent both fruitless and dangerous. No major urban protests followed the Tiananmen Square massacre, though tens of thousands of minor protests occurred in rural areas.

The United States was reminded of Chinese indifference to Western opinion regarding political matters during the 2012 Olympic Games. Chinese government officials announced that they would allow protests to occur in three parks in Beijing during the Games. Protesters were to be chosen based on an application process. The protests never occurred. The application process was merely a selection mechanism; those who applied were arrested. Journalists were told that if they wrote about the matter, they would be kicked out of the country.[68]

In order to understand the complicated economics behind the US-Chinese relationship, it's necessary to understand modern Chinese history and Chinese internal politics. Premier Wen, in his May 5, 2009, report to the People's Congress, said, "We must maintain sustained economic growth to mitigate the risks of social instability." The brunt of China's poverty and political injustice is felt in rural areas, where there are few government services, and residents are taxed highly despite earning incomes of

---

[67] Nicholas Kristof, "A Reassessment of How Many Died in the Military Crackdown in Beijing," New York Times, June 21, 1989.

[68] Financial Times, "Olympic Repression and a Gutless IOC: Promises, as Well as Records, Have Been Broken in Beijing," August 15, 2008.

$1,000/year or less. This encourages a continuous flow of population into China's cities, where political injustices are fewer and wages are higher, averaging over $4,000/year for manufacturing jobs. For the young, cities offer an escape from boredom, and, for males, a better chance of finding a mate (in some areas of China there are 140 men for every 100 women, a result of the one child policy).[69] The major problem facing the Chinese government is that growth must be high enough to accommodate most of the continuous influx of people seeking employment in the cities. Population flow into the cities acts as a sort of release valve for rural discontent. It also benefits the rural areas directly, as the newly employed people in the cities send large remittances back home.

The deeply symbiotic relationship between China and the United States—what Niall Ferguson has termed "Chimerica"—can be thought of as dating from 1978, when Deng Xiaoping became the paramount leader of the People's Republic of China.[70] Thirty-five years later, analysts are sharply divided on the sustainability of the US-Chinese economic relationship. In a balanced world, China would consume far more of its GDP and the United States would consume a bit less, and the current accounts that resulted would probably look more sustainable. The relationship between China and the United States in the last twenty-five years has unquestionably been mutually beneficial. The United States has been able to borrow at very low to negative real interest rates to fund consumption, and China has been able to grow its manufacturing base at a very high rate. China became, in

---

[69] Central Intelligence Agency, "Sex Ratios," The World Factbook, https://www.cia.gov/library/publications/the-world-factbook/fields/2018.html (accessed January 27 2013)

[70] Niall Ferguson, "Team 'Chimerica,'" Washington Post, November 17, 2011, http://www.washingtonpost.com/wp-dyn/content/article/2008/11/16/AR2008111601736.html (accessed January 27, 2013).

September 2008, the biggest holder of US Treasuries, and this is unlikely to reverse any time soon.[71] As of October 2012, China owns about $1.162 trillion in bills, notes, and bonds, according to the U.S. Treasury, remaining the largest holder of such debt.[72] The United States is the colossus of the world economy; in 2007, its current account deficit peaked at 70 percent as large as the cumulative account surpluses of all nations in surplus. By 2011, this figure has become a deficit of $465.9 billion, or about 30 percent of all global current account surpluses.[73] All of this turns traditional economic thinking, where capital flows from the developed to the developing world, on its head.

Even before the financial crisis hit, it was well known to economic observers that US budget deficits and US borrowing requirements were likely to be systematically high during 2008-2040 period. The first of the Baby Boomers began to collect Social Security in 2008. This massive cohort will fuel a dramatic increase in deficits if promised Medicare and Social Security benefits are delivered. China appears to be the most likely foreign source of funding for the resultant increase in US government borrowing. As of the end of 2008, China had 29 percent of the world's currency reserves (around $1.9 trillion total). Japan is dealing with a deepening crisis; they began reducing dollar-denominated debt holdings in December 2008. As of December 2011, China's reserves had increased to a

---

[71] US Treasury, Major Foreign Holders of Treasury Securities, http://www.treas.gov/tic/mfh.txt (accessed November 5, 2011). For a government view of the implications of China's holdings for the US economy, see Wayne M. Morrison and Marc Labonte, "CRS Report for Congress: China's Holdings of US Securities: Implications for the US Economy," Congressional Research Service, January 9, 2008, http://fpc.state.gov/documents/organization/99496.pdf (accessed November 5, 2011).

[72] US Treasury-Data Chart Center, International Accounts (accessed January 12, 2013).

[73] Central Intelligence Agency, The World Factbook, Country Comparisons. "Current Account Balance, 2011 est.," https://www.cia.gov/library/publications/the-world-factbook/rankorder/2187rank.html (accessed January 11, 2013).

formidable $3.2 trillion, which according to best estimates is about 60 percent US dollar–denominated, 10 percent Japanese yen–denominated, and a mix of the rest in pounds sterling- and euro- denominated.[76]

For the first time in a while, there is a question, not just of whether China will be willing to extend additional credit to the United States, but also whether it will able to. In 2011, total US output amounted to $15.08 trillion.[77] Total consumption by individuals, businesses, and government exceeded this figure by $459 billion. Of this, approximately $258 billion was financed by a drawdown on domestic savings, and $201 billion was borrowed from abroad. As of 2011, China owned about $1.2 trillion in bills, notes, and bonds, according to the US Treasury.[78]

The US situation is the result of what can perhaps be considered the slyest management of global economic arrangements in world history. For much of history, the dominant power did not pretend to be fair. The periphery was exploited for the benefit of the center. The current system of international trade, by contrast, is ostensibly the very picture of fairness. It is a system of mostly free trade and mostly flexible exchange rates. Such a system is intended to be fair intertemporally and across countries. It is ostensibly a level playing field where countries that have favorable trade balances should rapidly improve their lot. In theory, countries such as China that make sacrifices today to succeed in trade and save at high rates should be able to convert that discipline into high consumption in the future.

---

[76] People's Republic of China State Administration of Foreign Exchange, "China's Foreign Exchange Reserves, 1977–2011," Chinability, 2012 (accessed February 8, 2012), and People's Republic of China Internet Information Center, "China May Cut Its Dollar Holdings," September 12, 2008, http://www.china.org.cn/business/news/2008-09/12/content_16437985.htm (accessed February 8, 2013).

[77] World Economic Outlook Database, October 2012, International Monetary Fund (accessed January 12, 2013).

[78] US Treasury Data Chart Center, International Accounts (accessed January 12, 2013).

In reality, the world sometimes looks like, as Jacques Rueff once put it, "a childish game in which, after each round, the winners return their marbles to the losers."[79] As we have seen, in the twentieth century, when the dominant global economic arrangements became inconvenient for the United States, they would simply change the rules. If this pattern continues in the twenty-first century, we cannot expect that the United States will accept a role that will seem to its citizens like servitude to its creditor. That is, we cannot expect the United States to pay off its debts over time. Instead the situation will probably end up something akin to the new kid on the block who trades baseball cards with the neighborhood bully; if the bully ever finds out that the new kid got a good deal, he'll simply reverse the trade.

How would the United States "reverse the trade"? Broadly, it's fairly simple: the US assets that the Chinese hold are dollar-denominated US government bonds. Neither the bonds nor the dollars are backed by anything; they can both be inflated away. In practice, it's a bit more subtle than that. Since the loans that China has made to the United States are unbacked and are of fairly long duration, the United States has degrees of freedom in determining how it pays back its debt.[80] We can pay it sooner or later; we can inflate or not; we can manage our currency upwards or downwards. The Chinese don't have much freedom; the United States

---

[79] As quoted by Richard Duncan, The Dollar Crisis: Causes, Consequences, and Cures (New York: John Wiley & Sons, 2003), 23.

[80] The actual composition of the reserves is unknown. Brad Setser mentions in passing that China likely owns a lot of long-term debt. See Brad Setser, "Read Dean, Areddy and Ng on the Management of China's Reserves During the Crisis," Council on Foreign Relations Working Paper, January 30, 2009, http://www.economonitor.com/blog/2009/01/read-dean-areddy-and-ng-on-the-management-of-chinas-reserves-during-the-crisis/ (accessed November 5, 2011). Information on Chinese reserves can be found at Brad Setser and Arpana Pandey, "China's $1.7 Trillion Bet: China's External Portfolio and Dollar Reserves," Council on Foreign Relations Working Paper, January 2009, http://www.cfr.org/content/publications/attachments/CGS_WorkingPaper_6_China.pdf (accessed November 5, 2011).

basically determines how much real purchasing power the Chinese get back in exchange for their loans.

The Chinese strategy of investing its gains from international trade in dollar-denominated assets (mostly US government debt) was always a very questionable one. It had two primary motives. The first was to keep the dollar strong (arguably overvalued) and the yuan weak, so as to keep Chinese manufactured goods cheap in world markets and assure rapid growth of China's manufacturing sector. The second was to make China immune from the currency crises that have periodically disabled developing economies. China's large foreign reserves, coupled with its strict capital controls, make a sharp decline in the yuan nearly impossible. The problem with storing wealth in dollars is, first, that a successful developing economy will nearly always feature a currency that appreciates relative to established nations. Secondly, the United States has been, over the time that the Chinese have been accumulating debt, the very picture of financial irresponsibility, as voracious an accumulator of debt as the developed world has ever seen outside wartime. The dollar therefore was always destined to decline rapidly relative to the yuan. All of this ignores the possibility that, in their growth phase, the Chinese knew that the dollar-denominated investments they accumulated were in trouble, and accepted this as a cost of doing business. A disturbing part of the picture is that the counterpart to an undervalued yuan was an overvalued dollar. The expected result of this was a decimation of the US production of tradable goods and services. This made the Chinese policy of currency management self-defeating to some extent, as the decimation of the tradable goods sector in the United States makes it less likely that it will be able to pay off its debts in the long term.

On March 13, 2009, Premier Wen said, "We have lent a huge amount of money to the U.S. Of course we are concerned about the safety of our assets. To be honest, I am definitely a little worried." He called on the

United States to "maintain its good credit, to honor its promises and to guarantee the safety of China's assets."[81] This statement has a bit of the flavor of an undergrad asking a coed if she is on the pill after unprotected sex. The Chinese, although triumphant in trade, will still have to learn the lessons of the financial world in the usual way—that is, by getting fleeced a few times. The US government is likely to pursue the inflationary route over the next twenty years so as to ease the real burden of its national debt, though this will not solve the gargantuan problem going forward—that of funding entitlements, which are mostly specified in real terms.

China will likely diversify its international reserves away from dollars in the future. As it does so, it will be confronted with a psychological dilemma familiar to speculators everywhere. Such speculators will sometimes find that they have, unwisely, invested large amounts in a small, illiquid company. Suppose that this speculator has 100,000 shares of a five-dollar stock that trades 30,000 shares per day. The speculator finds it difficult to exit the position as the price declines, because he knows that his selling will cause a further decrease in price. He worries that the sale of any part of his position risks a negative cascade in price that could affect his remaining shares. This is roughly similar to the Chinese situation regarding Treasuries. Plenty of people are closely watching China's behavior regarding Treasuries, and any substantial sales (or even a sharp slowdown in purchases) could spark a negative cascade in either the dollar or the Treasury bond.

The Chinese like dollars because the rest of the world seems to go with them. It's a matter of faith. Part of the war of words between China and the United States stems from the fact that China knows that the United States knows that if it repudiates the dollar, the entire dollar regime is at

---

[81] Michael Wines, "China's Leader Says He Is 'Worried' Over US Treasuries," New York Times, March 13, 2009, http://www.nytimes.com/2009/03/14/business/worldbusiness/14china.html?_r=1 (accessed November 5, 2011).

risk. A move by China, the growing power, away from dollars and into other stores of wealth, be it another major currency or a basket of currencies or a new, asset-backed currency, would likely bring other countries along, and would be the beginning of the end of dollar dominance. China doesn't want to make such a move hastily, as a decline in dollar dominance would mean a decline in China's current wealth.

Nevertheless, China's public statements suggest that it plans to make such a move over the long term, and that it is willing to hasten that move if it believes that the United States is acting in a way that it deems financially irresponsible. It is not a coincidence that Premier Wen made his most public comments about US financial irresponsibility (in March 2009, at Davos) a short time after President Obama unveiled the generalities of his long-term budget plan at an address to a joint session of Congress on February 24, 2009.[83] China seems to have developed (late in the day, perhaps), a rational response function to US economic policy. If the United States pursues high-deficit, dollar-unfriendly policies, the Chinese threaten us with a move away from dollars and with the sale (or, at least, a refrain from new purchases) of US government debt. This hurts China by lowering their national wealth, but arguably hurts the United States more: if China steps away as lender, it's not clear who might take their place. Certainly other potential lenders will not be encouraged if China starts to back away. This is untenable for the United States, because in future years it needs, above all, to borrow. China's rational policy is to increase the threat of a move away from dollars in proportion to the perceived irresponsibility of US economic policy. At an extreme, where the perceived irresponsibility of

---

[83] Barack Obama, "Remarks of President Barack Obama—As Prepared for Delivery Address to Joint Session of Congress Tuesday, February 24th, 2009," http://www.whitehouse.gov/the_press_office/remarks-of-president-barack-obama-address-to-joint-session-of-congress/ (accessed November 5, 2011).

US policy is high, China figures to lose purchasing power rapidly whatever action it takes.

It seems to me that the evolution of the China-United States relationship going forward is mostly unpredictable. My sense is that, while China is correct in encouraging the United States to pursue responsible fiscal and monetary policies, and threatening to move away from dollars if the United States doesn't, it is unlikely that this jawboning will produce much tangible result. The jawboning would work if the United States ever faced the prospect of a failing government bond auction, but this is unlikely to happen, as the Federal Reserve is likely to create money to buy US Treasuries in the open market at whatever level is necessary. That the day of regular debt monetization of this kind will come, is, to me, a foregone conclusion. One could argue that we're already there.

My prediction therefore is that US actions will be mostly independent of China's desires, and China will suffer a decline in real wealth as a consequence. It is unclear to what extent this is expected among Chinese officials and to what extent it may come as a surprise. If it is indeed a surprise (it's hard to imagine that it can be fully a surprise), then we can expect mutually damaging retaliatory action. There are some indications that such retaliation could come in the form of China actively channeling natural resource trade (in oil and industrial commodities) away from the United States.

Given that US actions will be mostly independent of China's desires, the most relevant factor in the evolution of the relationship will be politics within the United States over the next couple of decades. Predictions about this are obviously hazardous, but in chapter 6 I suggest that politics in the United States is likely to move leftward. This is not likely to be good for either the US fiscal situation or the US-China relationship.

It's almost a given that China will gain in economic and political power relative to the United States in the next thirty years. The only thing that could prevent this is some kind of internal political implosion within China. Once China gains power, it is likely to be more protective of that power than the United States has been. China governs with the interest of the state in mind. China's assets were about 70 percent government-owned at their peak, with about 44 percent of all assets owned by SOEs, or State Owned Enterprises, today. It is worth noting that almost 50 percent of industrial-sector assets are state-owned.[84] The United States is governed in the interest of a collection of individuals whose desires sometimes accord with the interest of the state but often do not. It's a fundamental difference; in the United States, a ruler who intends to govern in the interest of the state is unlikely to get elected.

From a long-term perspective, the value of Chinese foreign currency reserves and other dollar-denominated wealth is not the country's major issue. This wealth is something like a stock variable, whereas the ongoing national income is a flow variable. It will be better for the Chinese to focus on the flow variable, even if it causes a diminution in the stock variable. As with an individual, if a country's income growth is strong, past wealth fades into insignificance. The big danger for China is not that it stands to lose a large fraction of its stored wealth but rather that it may struggle in the political arena and fall off the growth path entirely.

---

[84] Gao Xu, "State Owned Enterprises in China: How Big Are They?," Blog of the World Bank, http://blogs.worldbank.org/eastasiapacific/state-owned-enterprises-in-china-how-big-are-they (accessed January 27, 2013).

4 DEMOGRAPHICS AND THE ENTITLEMENT CRISIS

The entitlement crisis might be the biggest economic problem that we face, and yet few Americans have even the most basic understanding of it. To put it bluntly, the entitlement crisis in the United States is as simple as this: we need the programs in something like their current form, and yet we can't afford them. I believe that people hesitate to act on the entitlement issue for the same reasons that they hesitate on environmental matters: the problems play out over an extremely long time horizon, meaning that short-term issues always take precedence, and the problem is huge in magnitude, meaning that any implementable changes have little overall impact.

In 2008, each senior citizen received, on average, $27,000 in Social

Security, Medicare, and Medicaid benefits.[85] This figure looms large relative to per capita GDP ($46,500 in 2008).[86] When these programs were created, benefits were never intended to grow so large. The single biggest culprit has been escalating health care costs. A February 2012 analysis from the Center on Budget and Policy Priorities found that 53 percent of entitlements went to senior citizens (age 65-plus) in 2010.[87]

Medicare and Medicaid both work according to a fairly insane logic—they pay pretty much all health bills that come their way. Eligible program participants can consume almost any health care service they like, at no cost to themselves. This means that the costs of these programs grow not by some indexed cost of health care but rather by a higher number—whatever increase in costs can be justified by health care providers.

Social Security and Medicare are pay-as-you-go retirement systems; taxes paid by today's workers and their employers are used to pay the benefits of today's Social Security and Medicare recipients. The underlying demographic challenges confronting pay-as-you-go systems in the United States are fairly simple to understand. In 1955, there were 6.3 people aged 20–64 for every person over 65.[90] Someone who was 65 in 1955 could

---

[85] USA Today reported a number around $27,000: see Dennis Cauchon, "Senior Benefits Costs Up 24%: 'Health Care Crisis' Leads to 8-Year Rise," USA Today, February 14, 2008, http://www.usatoday.com/printedition/news/20080214/1a_lede14_dom.art.htm (accessed August 12, 2009). For more information, see Bryan M. Riedl, "A Guide to Fixing Social Security, Medicare, and Medicaid," Heritage Foundation,
http://www.heritage.org/research/budget/bg2114.cfm (accessed August 12, 2009).

[86] "National Income and Product Accounts Table: Table 1.1.5. Gross Domestic Product," Bureau of Economic Analysis,
http://www.bea.gov/national/nipaweb/TableView.asp?SelectedTable=5&FirstYear=2007&LastYear=2008&Freq=Qtr (accessed March 25, 2009); and "Population Finder," US Census Bureau, http://factfinder.census.gov/servlet/SAFFPopulation?_submenuId=population_0&_sse=on (accessed March 25, 2009).

[87] Sherman et al for the CBPP, "Contrary to 'Entitlement Society...,'" February 2012, http://www.cbpp.org/files/2-10-12pov.pdf (accessed January 12, 2013).

[90] Calculated from US Census Bureau, "Resident Population Plus Armed Forces Overseas—Estimates by Age, Sex, and Race: July 1, 1955," http://www.census.gov/popest/archives/pre-1980/PE-11-1955.pdf (accessed March 25, 2009).

expect to live for another 14 years.[91] In 2011, The U.S. Census showed there were 6.81 people aged 20-64 for every person over 65, and someone over 65 could expect to live another 19 years.[92] In 2030, it's projected that there will be 2.9 people aged 20–65 for every person over age 65, and 65-year-olds are expected to live to age 85.[93] The 2030 is likely conservative; many experts believe that there will be more dramatic gains in life expectancy by 2030 than projected, leading to much higher levels of Social Security and Medicare spending than projected.

The core demographic issues are a massive increase in life expectancy coupled with a decline in birth rates (25.1 births per 1,000 women in 1952 vs. 15.9 births per 1,000 women in 1980).[94] These issues increase the need for Social Security and Medicare, while making it substantially less likely that society will be able to afford the programs in anything like their current form. They increase the cost in the obvious way: starting around 2008, you have a relatively large generation (Baby Boomers) starting to draw retirement benefits, and they're expected to live for a long time.

It's fairly clear that recent demographic trends increase the need for Medicare and Social Security at the same time that they increase the costs of those programs. They do so in ways that are problematic and, therefore, infrequently discussed. First, people are limited in their ability to plan far

---

[91] National Center for Health Statistics, "Health, United States, 2007—With Chartbook on Trends in the Health of Americans" http://www.cdc.gov/nchs/data/hus/hus07.pdf#027 (accessed March 27, 2009). The values for 1950 and 1960 are 13.9 years and 14.3 years, respectively.

[92] US Census Bureau, "Age and Sex," 2012, http://www.census.gov/population/age/ (accessed January 27, 2013), and US Census Abstract, "Life Expectancy," 2012, http://www.census.gov/compendia/statab/cats/births_deaths_marriages_divorces/life_expectancy.html (accessed January 27, 2013).

[93] Social Security Administration, "2008 OASDI Trustees Report: Table V.A2-Intermediate Estimates," http://www.ssa.gov/OACT/TR/TR08/V_demographic.html#167717 (accessed March 27, 2009); see Table V.A4 for an average of male and female intermediate estimates.

[94] InformationPlease Database, "Live Births and Birth Rates," Pearson Education Group, http://www.infoplease.com/ipa/A0005067.html (accessed June 22, 2009).

into the future, and they are limited in their willingness to delay consumption today for the benefit of tomorrow. The net result is that, if people were required to fund their own retirement without government or family assistance, the vast majority would fail. It is difficult to accumulate the assets required to retire, and, even if one managed to accumulate them, it's difficult to hold onto them through death. The statistics are not encouraging. Sixty-five percent of the elderly have assets of less than the value of one year of nursing facility costs.[95] Laurence Kotlikoff, Ben Marx, and Pietro Rizza note that "41 percent of older SCF [the 2004 Survey of Consumer Finances] couples and 33 percent of SCF singles would experience a living standard reduction of 90 percent or more were Social Security benefits eliminated."[96]

Second, in one's seventies and eighties, medical expenses are both huge and unpredictable. If there were no government assistance, many families would be forced to choose between financial ruin and likely death of loved ones. Presumably, most of us would like to live in a country where a family is never put to that decision, no matter what sacrifices have to be made elsewhere in the economy, but it's also important to recognize that, as a society, we have chosen to extend life at all costs. In China, families often must make decisions that trade off cost against the likelihood of extending life.

Third, the fact that birth rates have decreased over time means that the elderly have fewer kids to care for them. Two other demographic issues that are relevant here: geographical mobility has gone up (increasing the distance

---

[95] Barbara Lyons et al., "The Distribution of Assets in the Elderly Population Living in the Community," The Kaiser Commission on Medicaid and the Uninsured (accessed June 22, 2009), http://www.kff.org/medicaid/loader.cfm?url=/commonspot/security/getfile.cfm&PageID=53591.
[96] Laurence J. Kotlikoff, Ben Marx, and Pietro Rizza, "Americans' Dependency on Social Security," NBER Working Paper No. 12696, November 2006, http://www.nber.org/papers/w12696 (accessed June 22, 2009).

between parent and child), and divorce rates are up (arguably, this decreases the psychological ties between parent and child).[97] Some have suggested that daughters are more likely to care for elderly parents than sons; clearly, lower birthrates mean a lower probability of having one or more daughters.[98]

In the United States, there is less flow of resources from parent to child than one might expect. There is also, perhaps less surprisingly, little flow of resources from children to parents. Laurence Kotlikoff and John Morris have found that transfers of income from child to parent are low, regardless of the income level of the child.[99]

The extent of the total unfunded liabilities in Social Security, Medicare, and Medicaid is somewhere around $45.9 trillion.[100] It is likely that this is an understatement, because the estimate includes estimates for life expectancy that are probably too low.[101] Unlike our national debt, which we can inflate

---

[97] See, for example, US Census Bureau, "Geographical Mobility: 2006 to 2007 Detailed Tables," http://www.census.gov/population/www/socdemo/migrate/cps2007.html (accessed August 12, 2009); US Census Bureau, "Domestic Net Migration in the United States: 2000 to 2004," http://www.census.gov/population/www/socdemo/migrate.html#estproj (accessed August 12, 2009); US Census Bureau, "Statistical Abstract of the United States: 2003—Table 83, 'Live Births, Deaths, Marriages, and Divorces: 1950 to 2001,'" http://www.census.gov/prod/2004pubs/03statab/vitstat.pdf (accessed August 12, 2009).

[98] Marvin B. Sussman, Suzanne K. Steinmetz, and Gary W. Peterson, eds., Handbook of Marriage and the Family (New York: Plenum Press, 1999), 432; Jane Gross, "Dividing Caregiving Duties, It's Daughters vs. Sons," New York Times, September 23, 2008, http://newoldage.blogs.nytimes.com/2008/09/23/in-the-nursing-home-its-daughters-v-sons/ (accessed August 12, 2009).

[99] Laurence J. Kotlikoff and John N. Morris, "How Much Care Do the Aged Receive From Their Children?: A Bimodal Picture of Contact and Assistance," NBER Working Paper No. W2391, February 1989, http://papers.ssrn.com/sol3/papers.cfm?abstract_id=314627 (accessed June 22, 2009).

[100] Kotlikoff and Burns, The Coming Generational Storm, 68. See also US Government Accountability Office, "Financial Statements of the United States Government for the Years Ended September 30, 2009 and 2008," http://www.gao.gov/financial/fy2009/09stmt.pdf (accessed June 3, 2010).

[101] Employee Benefit Research Institute, "Do the Social Security Projections Underestimate Future Longevity?: Both Job-Based Health Coverage and Uninsured Continue to Rise, CPS Shows," http://www.ebri.org/publications/notes/index.cfm?fa=notesDisp&content_id=3474 (accessed August 12, 2009); Andrew G. Biggs, "Good News on Social Security?," Christian Science Monitor, April 15, 2008, http://www.csmonitor.com/2008/0415/p09s02-coop.html (accessed August 12, 2009); Andrew G. Biggs, American Academy of Actuaries, "Wishful Thinking on Social Security,"

away to some extent,[102] our entitlement burden requires a real transfer of assets.[103]

There are many intelligent changes that one could make in the structure of entitlement programs. I won't review them in detail in this chapter for two reasons: they are unlikely to happen, and none of them makes much of a difference (it would be different if all were considered at once). The following are my proposed changes; I consider those first on the list to be more important and more urgent:

- Increase the retirement age (currently, 65 for Social Security and 67 for Medicare)
- Remove the cap on income subject to taxation for Social Security
    In 2013, whether someone made $600,000 or $6 million, he or she only paid payroll taxes for Social Security on the first $113,700.[104] This regressive system doesn't make a lot of sense in a world in which we desperately need more money for Social Security, Medicare, and Medicaid.

CATO Institute, http://www.cato.org/pub_display.php?pub_id=4481 (accessed August 12, 2009); "Assumptions Used to Project Social Security's Financial Condition," http://www.actuary.org/pdf/socialsecurity/assumptions_0104.pdf (accessed August 12, 2009).
[102] Kenneth Rogoff, "Embracing Inflation," Guardian, December 2, 2008, http://www.guardian.co.uk/commentisfree/cifamerica/2008/dec/02/global-economic-recession-inflation (accessed June 8, 2009); Richard Miller, "US Needs More Inflation to Speed Recovery, Say Mankiw, Rogoff," Bloomberg News, May 19, 2009, http://www.bloomberg.com/apps/news?pid=20601109&sid=auyuQIA1IRV8&refer=home (accessed June 8, 2009).

[103] Philip Glaser, "Inflation Versus Deflation: Part Two," http://viewfromthetower.wordpress.com/2008/12/17/inflation-versus-deflation-part-two/ (accessed August 12, 2009); Viviane Luporini, "Inflations Adjusted Nominal Deficit: A Note on Robert Barro's Definition," Universidade Federal de Minas Gerais, www.cedeplar.ufmg.br/pesquisas/td/TD%20138.doc (accessed August 12, 2009); Rui Zhao, "Money, Price and Output,"
https://netfiles.uiuc.edu/ruizhao/www/econ563/Lecture4_fiscal_theory_of_price.pdf (accessed August 12, 2009).

[104] Social Security Administration, "Contribution and Benefit Bases, 1937–2013," http://www.ssa.gov/OACT/COLA/cbb.html (accessed January 27, 2013).

- Eliminate some of the nonessential procedures covered by Medicare and Medicaid

    Should Medicaid really cover braces?
- Engage in tort reform

    Medicare and Medicaid indirectly pay for the massive legal liability that is endemic to the health care profession.
- Improve some of the more egregious incentive problems with the current Social Security set-up

    Widows have almost no incentive to work in the current system, since the income they earn from work lowers the Social Security benefits they inherit from their spouse.

The entitlement crisis presents the following problem: the deeper you dig, the worse it looks. As bad as the underlying economics and demographics are, the politics are worse. At around 11:30 p.m. on June 27, 2003, the House of Representatives began voting on the Medicare Prescription Drug, Improvement, and Modernization Act; after the fifteen minutes usually required to complete a vote, it was apparent that the tally had Republicans short of the majority of votes they needed to send the bill to the Senate.[105] Why did the vote come up short? One reason is that almost every analyst who considered the bill thought it to be horrendous policy. It was thought simply to cost too much for the benefits conferred.

One aspect of the bill that analysts found particularly offensive was that the government was prohibited from negotiating prices directly with drug companies. The story behind this bill was evident to most observers. President Bush was seeking insurance of sorts for his 2004 reelection

---

[105] Henry J. Aaron, "Prescription Drug Bill: The Good, the Bad, and the Ugly," Brookings Institution, http://www.brookings.edu/articles/2004/0115useconomics_aaron.aspx?rssid=washington+dc (accessed March 27, 2009).

campaign. The pharmaceutical lobby was powerful enough to coax Bush and members of Congress into prohibiting negotiation on drug prices—an obviously ridiculous provision, as Medicare recipients are a large and increasing percentage of the overall prescription drug market.[106] The House of Representatives, despite being almost completely under the sway of the White House, saw this bill as so egregious that some members staged a revolt and refused to pass it.

But the House leadership refused to accept nonpassage of the bill. House Speaker Dennis Hastert held the vote open for almost three hours past the standard close, a move pulled only once in the previous twenty years (by Jim Wright, in 1987).[107] During this time, the House leadership presumably browbeat junior members into changing their votes. The bill passed, 216–215, at 2:33 a.m. (with Democratic representatives running back to try to vote), and was signed into law on December 8, 2003.[108]

Strenuous efforts of this type to provide for the aged and aging are not unique to the United States. Everywhere, the superior economic and political resources of the older members of society translate into favorable legislative treatment. It's not too much of an exaggeration to say that the political and economic history of the past sixty years in Argentina has been

---

[106] For the power of the pharmaceutical/healthcare lobby, see R. Jeffrey Smith and Jeffrey H. Birnbaum, "Drug Bill Demonstrates Lobby's Pull: Democrats Feared Industry Would Stall Bigger Changes," Washington Post, January 12, 2007, http://www.washingtonpost.com/wp-dyn/content/article/2007/01/11/AR2007011102081.html (accessed August 12, 2009).

[107] Jonathan Chait, The Big Con: Crackpot Economics and the Fleecing of America (New York: Houghton Mifflin, 2007), 201; John A. Ferrell, Tip O'Neill and the Democratic Century (Boston: Back Bay Books, 2001), 637; Ellen Miller, "When the Tables Were Turned," http://tpmcafe.talkingpointsmemo.com/2005/10/07/when_the_tables_were_turned/ (accessed August 12, 2009).

[108] "H.R. 1—108th Congress (2003): Medicare Prescription Drug, Improvement, and Modernization Act of 2003," GovTrack.us, http://www.govtrack.us/congress/bill.xpd?bill=h108-1 (accessed March 27, 2009).

dominated by an intergenerational war between young and old.[109] (The old mostly won, bankrupting the economy on numerous occasions.)

If you don't see an intergenerational war today in the United States, you are not looking hard enough. All forms of bailouts and asset price protection measures that we have seen have a heavy intergenerational component. The monstrous federal debt we are incurring to undertake these bailouts must be paid back! It is the younger generations that will bear the tax burden (or the more hellish reality of a bankrupted government). Most of the benefits of the bailouts occur to the old, as they are the ones who own the majority of the equity and the debt attached to the companies and assets being bailed out.[110] Measures to artificially increase home prices involve tax dollars (to be paid in the future, of course, not now) and also have an intergenerational component—increased home prices benefit those who already have a home but hurt those who do not yet have one.

Government tax receipts as a percentage of GDP averaged eighteen percent from 1944 to 2003, with a standard deviation of only 1.27 percent.[111] Entitlements are a very long-term problem, and tax rates affect long-term growth rates in unpredictable ways, so it's hard to say how far tax rates will have to increase to keep US government finances from going critical. (The debt becomes "critical" when the costs of servicing it are

---

[109] Jorge Bravo, "Intergenerational Transfers and Social Protection in Latin America," paper presented at the Economic Commission for Latin America and the Caribbean, 2005, http://www.un.org/esa/population/meetings/Proceedings_EGM_Mex_2005/bravo.pdf (accessed June 30, 2009);

Blustein, And the Money Kept Rolling In (And Out).

[110] See, for example, Federal Reserve Board, "2007 Survey of Consumer Finances," http://www.federalreserve.gov/pubs/oss/oss2/2007/scf2007home.html (accessed March 27, 2009); Peter S. Yoo, "Age Distributions and Returns of Financial Assets," Federal Reserve Bank of St. Louis http://research.stlouisfed.org/wp/1994/94-002.pdf (accessed August 12, 2009).

[111] Kotlikoff and Burns, 178; "Total Federal Revenues: 1900–2003 (Percent of GDP)," CATO Institute, http://www.cato.org/research/fiscal_policy/2002/growth1.html (accessed June 2, 2009).

sufficiently high relative to GDP that it becomes impossible to prevent the debt from exploding upwards.) We know that fairly large changes are required; to maintain current benefit levels, we could increase tax receipts to 25 or 30 percent of GDP and still have to increase our ratio of national debt to GDP over time. Note that, with government receipts averaging 18 percent over the past sixty years, we've only managed to keep our government finances just shy of the critical phase despite favorable demographics; government outlays have averaged almost 21 percent of GDP during the same period.[112]

It's often argued that our finances are not near critical in 2013 and that we in fact have plenty of room to grow our ratio of debt to GDP. These arguments most commonly point out that, among the ten wealthiest countries, only China and Brazil have a lower ratio of federal debt to GDP.[113] My first reaction to this is a plea to common sense—if you don't foresee that you will ever be able to pay off your current debt based on your current debt levels, your projected expenses, and your earning capacity, does it make you feel better that your friends have a higher ratio of debt-to-income than you do?

Although the federal debt-to-GDP measure is flawed—a proper metric should also consider implicit debt (such as promised entitlement payments)—it's true that many of world's richest economies are confronting similar problems. The demographics and politics we've explored are more extreme in Japan and Europe than they are in the United

---

[112] Calculated from "Budget of the United States: Historical Tables Fiscal Year 2005," http://www.gpoaccess.gov/usbudget/fy05/hist.html (accessed August 12, 2009). Outlays averaged 20.77 percent of GDP from 1940 to 2003.

[113] Central Intelligence Agency, The World Factbook, "Country Comparison: Public Debt," https://www.cia.gov/library/publications/the-world-factbook/rankorder/2186rank.html (accessed January 27, 2013).

States.[114] That said, concluding that the United States is in good shape relative to Japan and Europe because its debt-to-GDP ratio is moderate is premature. First, the ratio of debt to GDP is a good metric to use for Denmark or Belgium but a bad measure to use when your GDP is $15 trillion and your federal debt is $16 trillion.[115] The absolute size of your borrowing need is relevant. Note also that the problem is actually exacerbated, not helped, by the fact that it is shared by other countries—the debt markets are going to be crowded for the next fifty years or so. Secondly, the United States has problems competing in the world economy; or, rather, it has problems getting the world to buy enough of its products to cover its prodigious demand for imports. The United States has been running large current account deficits for thirty years.[116] A country cannot pay off its debts to the rest of the world if it persistently runs current account deficits. Thirdly, the United States has a low national savings rate.[117] This is closely related to its continued current account deficits. A country that loads itself with debt while saving little and running persistent current account deficits is simply asking for a crisis.

Our economy could not withstand the tax rates that would be necessary to maintain our entitlement programs in anything like their current form and keep the debt from going critical. Whatever might be said of Obama's specific policies, he is getting the big picture right by, first,

---

[114] For debt and demographic information, see Central Intelligence Agency, The World Factbook https://www.cia.gov/library/publications/the-world-factbook/ (accessed January 27, 2013).

[115] "National Income and Product Accounts Table: Table 1.1.5. Gross Domestic Product"; "The Debt to the Penny and Who Holds It," TreasuryDirect, http://www.treasurydirect.gov/NP/BPDLogin?application=np (accessed January 27, 2013).

[116] "US International Transactions Accounts Data: Table 1. US International Transactions," Bureau of Economic Analysis Interactive Data, http://www.bea.gov/iTable/index_ita.cfm (accessed January 27, 2013).

[117] See "National Income and Product Accounts Tables: Table 5.1. Saving and Investment," Bureau of Economic Analysis Interactive Data, http://www.bea.gov/iTable/index_nipa.cfm (accessed January 27, 2013)

increasing payroll taxes and preparing the American people for higher taxes in the future, and, second, making it known that the long-term health of Medicare is shaky and that we will lose it sooner rather than later if we don't rein in the rapid growth of health care expenses.

5 THE ECONOMIC SIGNIFICANCE OF CULTURAL DECLINE

The tone of our national debate is typically formal and self-righteous. We focus on cold, big-picture variables: budget deficits, unemployment numbers, stock prices. Few commentators bother to tackle the big, messy questions about culture. Still, it seems reasonable to ask the question: Is it possible that, culturally, we're a bit too messed-up to mind the store? Three cultural trends relevant to our past and future economic paths would seem to indicate that we might be: first, a shortened attention span, when the complexity of our economy is increasing at a rapid clip; second, a decline in savings rates (broadly construed); and, third, a decline in societal trust levels.

As James Gleick says, entertainment and communication get "faster" every year by most measures—beats per minute, frames per second.[118] What implications does this faster world have for our long-run economic capacity? A faster world, characterized by more general "noise" per unit of time, can diminish overall productive capacity in two main respects. First, it can crowd out mental energy that could be used in productive ways. Second, it can lessen our tolerance for what moves slower. It's astonishing how far the process can go—one may feel that voice communication is too "slow," for instance, and prefer texting. Some of us could never have envisioned such a change. Still, from the perspective of individuals, the decline in attention span that has come with a faster world may have both positive and negative effects: our newly limited ability to concentrate may act like a governor on the "happiness treadmill," with adjustments assuring that none of us has "too good" or "too bad" a time. Yet from the perspective of the nation as a whole, our every-shortening attention span negatively affects our long-run economic capability. It's likely it also affects our plasticity—the ability of the economy to respond to negative/adverse shocks.

While in theory the impressive improvements in digital communication and social media of the past decade should lead to substantial improvements in our ability to coordinate complex productive activity, in fact they seem to lead to a fractalization of concern with the self. We're documenting and sharing our own lives at a faster pace; we live in an age of cultural hyperinflation. What you get, at the end of the day, is a frenetic but listless population. We're wrecking our attention spans at a time when we need them, more than ever before, to tackle the relentless complexity of the modern economy.

---

[118] James Gleick, Faster: The Acceleration of Just About Everything (New York: Pantheon Books, 1999).

Let's relate the decline in the American savings ethic to an unusual phenomenon: the increase in the popularity of tattoos in the United States. While time-series data in this realm leave much to be desired, crude measurements indicate that the trend is real. A 1936 study found that 6 percent of people were tattooed; the number has risen to around 15 percent in the past decade.[119] The number of women with tattoos quadrupled between 1960 and 1980.[120] While no one listed in *People* magazine's 1980 "Who is the most beautiful woman?" survey had a tattoo, seven of the ten women listed by the international men's monthly *FHM* as "sexiest women in the world" in 2008 did.[121]

Are tattoos—ironically, in spite of their permanence—a credible signal that one lives for today? In many social contexts, it's valuable to portray the image that you are the kind of person who lives for the moment. A tattoo serves as a signaling device. It is sufficiently costly that it creates a separating equilibrium—it allows those who live for the day to credibly convey that fact. Is it a stretch to relate the number of tattoos to the declining US savings rate? I will throw the rise in obesity into the mix as well. Among American adults between twenty-four and seventy, the percentage of those who are overweight jumped from 44.8 percent in 1960 to 66 percent in 2004, with those being obese increasing from 13.3 percent to 32.1 percent during the same period.[122] By 2012, 35.7 percent of US

---

[119] Anna Swan, "Tattoo Statistics," Associated Content, http://www.associatedcontent.com/article/31975/tattoo_statistics.html?cat=7 (accessed August 14, 2009).

[120] "Infinite Tattoos Blog," http://infinitetattoos.wordpress.com/2008/07/ (accessed August 14, 2009).

[121] "100 Sexiest Women in the World 2008," FHM, July 2008.

[122] "Statistics Related to Overweight and Obesity," US Department of Health and Human Services, http://www.win.niddk.nih.gov/publications/PDFs/stat904z.pdf (accessed August 14, 2009).

adults and 16.9 percent of children qualified as obese.[123] Excluding the percentage of those whose obesity has a medical provenance, the increase may be said to point to something like the same shortsightedness: obesity is a consequence of a lifestyle while tattoos are an advertisement of it, but the phenomenon at heart is the same.

For economists of the Austrian school, GDP statistics are fairly meaningless as a measure of economic progress. The important thing is not level of economic output but rather the proportion of output devoted to investment as compared with the portion that is consumed. Investment increases long-run economic capacity; consumption represents a drawdown of economic assets and therefore represents a depletion of long-run capacity. Needless to say, economists of the Austrian school are not pleased with recent US economic trends. Their thinking can also be applied to the world of human capital. A week in the library represents an investment in human capital; a week drinking beer at the beach represents consumption, or a decrease in human capital. The United States is not depleting its human capital in a massively irresponsible way, but I'd suggest that to the extent that human capital accumulation is a competition, we have been losing ground, and perhaps at a increasing rate.

The problem within the United States is not only an underaccumulation of human capital but also misdirection in the investment of human capital. As Pacific Investment Management (PIMCO) co-founder Bill Gross says, "Something is wrong when there's a shortage of computer engineers and an oversupply of financial engineers." Financial bubbles push too much talent in one direction, as was true with technology and Internet-related

---

[123] Tara Parker-Pope, "Obesity Rates Stall in US but Stay Stubbornly High," New York Times, January 18, 2012.

businesses during the dot-com bubble. In economic terms, the United States suffers from a subjective discount rate that is too high, in both real capital accumulation and human capital accumulation. To a greater extent than is good, we value current consumption over future consumption. This is very likely a matter of preference—Americans are expressing a preference for current consumption, and any move to a higher savings regime might well lower overall utility, which includes today's utility plus the discounted value of all future utility. So, as in previous examples, the United States might be behaving rationally from the standpoint of economics, yet in a way that is detrimental to its long-term economic health.

Francis Fukuyama argues, in *Trust: The Social Virtues and the Creation of Prosperity*, that the level of trust is a forgotten variable in macroeconomics and has substantial power in explaining the structure, evolution, and performance of particular economies.[124] The US economy, in Fukuyama's view, ranked very high in trust. In the United States, people trust not only their extended family but also, sometimes, those they have just met; this general amicability, which might lead to two people who meet in a bar one night starting a business together the following week, has been a source of dynamism and strength for the United States in the world economy.

The long downturn that started in 2008 will result in substantial declines in the overall level of trust in US society. It is simply a matter of how far trust levels will fall. High levels of unemployment and generally tenuous employment situations will be a leading factor in the fall in trust. The grossly unequal distribution of wealth and income in the United States is less of a problem when most people's incomes are growing and people feel

---

[124] Francis Fukuyama, Trust: The Social Virtues and the Creation of Prosperity (New York: Simon & Schuster, 1995).

that the economy is strong and fluid. In such an environment, upward mobility is a palliative for otherwise unacceptable levels of inequality. During a sharp and prolonged recession, mobility is stunted and inequality becomes sharply apparent because the wealthy, although they might have suffered huge losses, still have a cushion to support them through hard times. The poor and middle class feel, justifiably, that the brunt of the downturn is borne by them.

We've lived through a time where rent-seeking in the economy—manipulating the current environment to gain wealth, as opposed to creating new value—reached unheard-of levels (the financial sector peaked at 42 percent of total US corporate profits in 2006); the benefits of this rent-seeking accrued to those who ensconced themselves in power in financial firms.[125] So much of these firms' capital bases had been paid to employees that, for the financial sector as a whole, equity was possibly negative in fall 2008, just two and a half years after the beginning of the (predictable) fall in housing prices.

The US government led a banking sector recapitalization of unprecedented proportions. The details of the bailouts began coming to light in the year or two after they occurred. The language of bailouts and emergency measures acts insidiously to destroy trust levels. Very often, we heard policymakers remark that this or that bailout had to happen because, whatever the long-term cost of the bailout, it was outweighed by the risk of catastrophe in the near term. What this language does, with respect to trust levels, is to shorten everyone's time horizons; if government officials are implying that tomorrow doesn't matter as much because we might not get

---

[125] "Greed and Fear," Economist, January 22, 2009,
http://www.economist.com/members/survery_paybarrier.cfm?issue=20090124 (accessed April 17, 2009).

there, then sooner or later, this short-term frame of mind is going to seep into everyday individual interactions.

Consider the opening of Robert Axelrod's *The Evolution of Cooperation*: "Under what conditions will cooperation emerge in a world of egoists without central authority?" Axelrod suggests that the crucial requirement is repeated interaction. In short-term interactions, people tend to defect toward their own short-term interest.[126] In a *Mad Max*–type world, where human interactions are random and short-lived, we can expect harsh interaction. Unwittingly, government officials, in their policy justifications and in their manner of speech, are creating a shorter-horizon mode of decision making that will tend to cause dissolution of trust in some measure.

In making the case for his proposed health care program to the public on July 22, 2009, President Obama emphasized that the status quo was unacceptable, and implied that without a major, centrally directed change, medical costs would soar uncontrollably over time, severely straining individuals and breaking Medicare and Medicaid. In framing his case in these terms, he created anxiety and fear about the future. Arguably, the effect of these emotions is to shorten people's overall decision-making horizon, creating a lower-trust society.

***

Robert Putnam's *Bowling Alone*, an extensive documentation of antisocial behavior and the decline of civic organizations, described a sense of nostalgia for the communitarian ethic of the past but little real longing to recreate community in the modern era.[127] The psychologist Mihaly Csikszentmihalyi notes that people enjoy time with family but tend to enjoy time with friends more, and enjoy times of "flow" most of all—times when

---

[126] Robert Axelrod, The Evolution of Cooperation (New York: Basic Books, 2006).
[127] Robert Putnam, Bowling Alone: The Collapse and Revival of American Community (New York: Simon & Schuster, 2000).

they are fully immersed in activities, often solitary, that they are extremely passionate about.[128] The modern human in wealthy societies is constantly in search of these high-intensity "flow" experiences, and the suffering of (essentially more boring) community activity is a consequence.

The observed behavior of modern, rich societies suggests that this fracturing of community, in favor of a society where individuals are more free to pursue their own conception of optimal experiences, can go a very long way. The wealthier a society, it seems, the fewer the counterweights toward individualism. Communitarian restrictions provided by history, religion, and family ties are more often than not simply cast aside.

Although some of the consequences of individualism are regrettable, it might well be the case that our current fractured, individualistic, short-horizon society is optimal in terms of cumulative overall happiness. In the absence of a comprehensive framework/philosophy that suggests how life should be lived, for better or worse, in early twenty-first century Western nations, we have adopted the moral philosophy of the economist: the best course of action is that which maximizes the sum of happiness of individuals.

In the long term, the United States is following the playbook of a failed empire. This playbook consists of a weak political will abroad, an unsustainable trade balance, increasing public debt (to the point where default or very high inflation is inevitable), a declining culture (at least in terms of fundamental cultural variables associated with economic performance), the financialization of the economy and its influence on rent-seeking activity, and—finally—an inability as a nation to make difficult, long-term political choices. What's the appropriate strategy when you're

---

[128] Mihaly Csikszentmihalyi, Flow: The Psychology of Optimal Experience (New York: HarperCollins, 2008).

going through a financial crisis in the midst of a broader, long-run decline? We haven't figured that out yet.

Where does this leave us? Complexity in the system will likely have to decrease; we're no longer capable, culturally, of holding things together in the current form. It's an uphill battle, fought against natural resource constraints, unfavorable demographics, and treacherous government finances, and we're just not up for it. What's likely is that a communitarian ethic will assert itself in the United States and other rich nations out of necessity; widespread failings at the macro level will force people to pay increased attention to their immediate environment.

6 THE PERILS OF REDISTRIBUTION

It is easy to forget that times of reversal or stagnation are at least as common as times of economic progress in human history. The shift in economic thought that occurred in the second half of the twentieth century from an emphasis on political economy to an emphasis on pure economics is unfortunate. The reason that economic progress stalls or reverses is not because people forget the advances they've made in the production and distribution of goods and services; it is because people suffer reversals in how well they get along with one another.

On both the political and economic fronts, it should be evident that turbulent times are ahead. We are going through intense social, economic, political, intergenerational, international, and economic rebalancing, all at the same time. Perhaps it's always been so; but I can't think of another period when so many problems came to a head at once.

One reason that capitalism and democracy work well together is that democracy allows the voting populace to blunt the harsher aspects of capitalism by voting in politicians who are likely to enact redistributive policies. Some observers contend that capitalism would not have survived the postwar years in Europe if not for a somewhat rapid move toward redistributive policies. The populace continuously wields the threat of redistributive policies over the wealthy, and this at least theoretically constrains the wealthy and powerful in good times.

But therein also lies the system's weakness. A recognized flaw of democratic capitalism is that people can vote themselves wealth. In a pure democracy, someone could propose a referendum enacting, say, a 50 percent wealth tax on the wealthiest 1 percent of the population, and, if the referendum passed, such a wealth distribution would be attempted.

It's possible that the United States is entering a phase of its history where a relatively rapid redistribution of wealth is necessary to save our economic system. We might have reached a point where a large number of people want the current system torn apart, even if it means pain in the interim. As my friend Brian Finn puts it, there is a danger that "people are going to look at their foreclosed house, their nonexistent 401k, and they are going to be like, 'Fuck it, I don't want to play this game anymore. It's worked for others but not for me. Whatever the old rules were, I'm not going to follow them.'"

Given the nature of our political system, redistributive policies will happen whether they are a good idea or not, if a majority of people want them. Yet they would be a disaster in the United States from a purely economic point of view. Socialism works in Scandinavia because it has a small, homogeneous population with a deeply ingrained egalitarian ethic. By contrast, socialist policies in the United States are likely to be gamed to the maximum extent. In the United States, if you give people almost as much money for not working as for working, they will not work. Rather than an egalitarian ethic, the ethic in the United States is to maximize one's personal well-being, provided that one is playing by the rules. This is not a terrible thing; a libertarian ethic of this sort makes for a free, and frankly enjoyable, social arrangement. It is, however, not the ideal backdrop for implementing leftist policy.

One case for redistribution is that the economic structure of a country is a function of that country's distribution of wealth. A country that is highly stratified economically, with some who are very rich and many who are very poor, cannot expect to have a well-developed network of businesses servicing the needs of the middle class. Things like efficient grocery store chains and high-quality consumer products are usually not produced in countries without a middle class. This seemingly creates an argument for transferring money from rich to poor.

The problem is that the wealth and income distribution in the United States is so unequal that much of our economy, especially in our major cities, has been organized around providing for the wants of the rich.[129] It's been this way for so long that we cannot quickly change course. The economic structure of places like New York City simply doesn't work if you don't have a lot of people who have huge amounts of after-tax money to spend.

Taxes in the United States are already among the most progressive in the world.[130] As of January 2013, a single professional in New York City

---

[129] Carmen DeNavas-Walt, Bernadette D. Proctor, and Jessica C. Smith, "Income, Poverty, and Health Insurance Coverage in the United States: 2007," US Census Bureau, http://www.census.gov/prod/2008pubs/p60-235.pdf (accessed April 17, 2009); for an international comparison, see "Inequality in Income or Expenditure," UNDP Human Development Report 2007/2008, http://hdrstats.undp.org/indicators/ (accessed April 17, 2009).

[130] Worldwide-Tax.com , "Tax Rates Around the World," http://www.worldwide-tax.com/index.asp#partthree (accessed August 16, 2009); Worldwide-Tax.com, "US Tax Laws and

earning $500,000 would pay a federal tax rate of 39.6 percent (marginal rate), a state tax rate of 6.85 percent, and a city tax rate of $1,706 plus 3.648 percent of income over $50,000.[131] Progressive tax systems have a dangerous sort of operating leverage, by which small declines in income can mean huge changes in tax revenue. To see this, imagine a tax structure of the most progressive sort, one where there were no taxes on incomes up to $100,000, but any income beyond that point was taxed at 50 percent. If income in such a system drops 20 percent—from, say, $140,000 to $112,000—tax revenue drops 70 percent, from $20,000 to $6,000. In 2008, Nicole Gelinas noted that "the city's coffers will see even sharper drops, because our progressive system makes us acutely dependent on the rich, not the middle class, to pay our bills. As an example, when income fell just 1.2 percent from 2001 to 2002, tax revenues dropped by nearly 7%."[132]

President Obama has made it clear that he would like to increase the progressiveness of the tax system. The case for doing so seems compelling. During an October 2008 speech titled "The Future of Market Capitalism," Larry Summers invited listeners to compare the income distribution of the United States now with the distribution in 1979.[133] He

---

Tax System," http://www.worldwide-tax.com/us/us_taxes.asp (accessed August 16, 2009).

[131] Tax Foundation, "US Federal Individual Income Tax Rates History, 1913–2012," http://www.taxfoundation.org/taxdata/show/151.html (accessed January 15, 2013); Tax Foundation, "State Individual Income Tax Rates, 2000–2012," http://www.taxfoundation.org/taxdata/show/228.html (accessed January 15, 2013). For New York City, the 2012 values come from NYC Finance 2012, "Tax year 2009 Personal Income tax brackets," http://taxes.about.com/gi/o.htm?zi=1/XJ&zTi=1&sdn=taxes&cdn=money&tm=8&f=10&su=p284.1 3.342.ip_p504.6.342.ip_&tt=2&bt=1&bts=1&st=36&zu=http%3A//www.nyc.gov/html/dof/html/pd f/interest_rates/pitrates.pdf (accessed January 15, 2013).

[132] Nicole Gelinas, "NYC's Debt Disaster," New York Post, September 23, 2008, http://www.nypost.com/seven/09232008/postopinion/opedcolumnists/nycs_debt_disaster_13032 2.htm (accessed April 17, 2009).

[133] Larry Summers, "The Future of Market Capitalism," paper presented at Harvard Business School's Global Business Summit, October 14, 2008, http://ksghome.harvard.edu/~lsummer/08.10.16_HBS_Global_Summit_Keynote.pdf (accessed April 17, 2009).

said, "If you do that, you will find that the share of income going to those in the 80th to 99th percentiles has stayed about the same. Those in the top 1% of the income distribution have gained about six hundred billion dollars. Those in the bottom 1% have lost about six hundred billion."[134] This is admittedly quite an injustice, and part of the Obama platform is to reverse it. That said, increasing progressiveness will increase the dependence of federal government inflows on the incomes of the very rich, at the same time that it is discouraging effort from that group. This seems to me like a backward-looking policy. The world has changed since 2007, when the financial sector, the source of many of the highest incomes, accounted for 40 percent of US corporate profits.[135]

Although the Laffer curve is about as far as one can get from the current intellectual fashion in Washington, D.C., one should appreciate that although Laffer's simple diagram was misapplied to justify poor tax policy, the essential truth remains: government tax revenue increases at a decreasing rate as the tax rate is increased, then at some point it begins falling.[136] We don't know what the revenue-maximizing level of tax rates is, but I contend that for the top income bracket, it is somewhere around 60 percent.

We aren't that far from 60 percent right now. Consider also that "revenue-maximizing" is a long way from optimal. The optimal tax rate would surely be lower, as the development of new business enterprises would be stunted at the rate that maximizes tax revenue in the short term. State and local government finances are in terrible shape. We can

---

[134] Ibid.

[135] "Greed and Fear," Economist, January 22, 2009.

[136] Arthur B. Laffer, "The Laffer Curve: Past, Present, and Future," Heritage Foundation http://www.heritage.org/Research/Taxes/bg1765.cfm (accessed April 17, 2009).

expect that tax rates will increase significantly in both states and municipalities, and they will do so in a progressive way. The top marginal tax rate in New York is approximately 8.82 percent (for a total tax burden of a "single" filing NYC resident in the top bracket of 46 percent). In California, it's 10.3 percent at the state level.[137] Property taxes typically amount to 2–4 percent of income (up to almost 8 percent in parts of NY) and are also likely to go up.[138]

The richest 10 percent of Americans account for about 70 percent of all US personal income tax revenue.[139] Increasing the top rate by 1 percent would likely raise about $60 billion in incremental revenue annually. That is a decent sum, but it is hardly a trace when compared to the $3.39 trillion[140] the federal government plans to spend in 2013, especially when considering that most bailouts are done outside the budget. Subsequent increases in tax rates would yield smaller and smaller increases in government revenue. If you increased the top federal rate by 10 percent, bringing it to somewhere near 60 percent in states with high taxes, you would increase federal receipts by something like $400 billion. This is not a large sum, and it would change behavior in unfavorable ways that would affect long-term government

---

[137] Tax Foundation, "State Individual Income Tax Rates," http://taxfoundation.org/article/state-individual-income-tax-rates-2000-2012 (accessed January 12, 2013).

[138] Tax Foundation, "Property Tax on Owner-Occupied Housing, by County, Ranked by Property Taxes as a Percentage of Home Vale, 2006–2008 Average," http://taxfoundation.org/article/property-tax-owner-occupied-housing-county-ranked-property-taxes-percentage-home-value-2006-2008-3 (accessed January 12, 2013).

[139] Tax Foundation, "US Federal Individual Income Tax Rates History, 1913–2010;" William McBride, "Summary of Latest Federal Individual Income Tax Data," http://www.taxfoundation.org/news/show/250.html (accessed January 12, 2013), and http://taxfoundation.org/blog/no-country-leans-upper-income-households-much-us (accessed January 12, 2013). On average, the top-bracket individuals pay an effective tax rate of 22.79 percent, even though they fall in the 35 percent bracket.

[140] Budget of the United States Government: Fiscal Year 2009, Summary Tables, http://www.gpoaccess.gov/usbudget/fy09/pdf/budget/tables.pdf (accessed January 12, 2013).

revenue. High tax rates encourage people to work less, invest less, and move more of their activities underground.

Wealth taxes will probably be seriously discussed at some point in the next five years. This seems obvious based on the fact that all forms of government finance are facing tremendous shortfalls, and wealth looms large relative to income as a potential source of government revenue. There is a lot of wealth in the United States, and most of it is very concentrated. The top 1 percent control over a third of the national wealth.[141] Legal scholars seem to agree that a federal wealth tax would be unconstitutional. Wealth taxes, however, are constitutional in most states, and Florida had one until recently. At the local level, property taxes can be viewed as a form of wealth tax.

Wealth taxes can be considered a last resort, as they're very much against the capitalist way of doing things, but we've reached a time where last resorts need to be considered. They're an easy sell politically, as those taxes targeting wealth above a certain (high) level are the most progressive available.

Critics suggest that wealth taxes represent a repudiation of private property rights and that this represent a slippery slope toward no private wealth. We can dismiss slippery slope arguments out of hand, noting that every non-corner policy solution is a slippery solution toward something, and we can dismiss the property rights argument by noting that income taxes, also, are a repudiation of private property rights. The government could have just as well given you the income untaxed, had you buy

---

[141] G. William Domhoff, 'Wealth, Income and Power," http://sociology.ucsc.edu/whorulesamerica/power/wealth.html (accessed August 16, 2009). Domhoff indicates that, as of 2004, the top 1 percent controlled 34.3 percent of the aggregate net worth and 42.2 percent of the financial wealth. He cites E. N. Wolff, Changes in Household Wealth in the 1980s and 1990s in the U.S. (2004), unpublished manuscript.

something with it, then taken that from you. That is just the way government works.

Many of the very wealthy in this country would obviously be anxious about the prospect of a wealth tax, but many of them are also quite comfortable with the prospect of higher taxes and stronger regulations. Why wouldn't they be? They are already rich; they might as well protect this system. Let the young who are coming up pay for it.

Another way to alter the distribution of wealth in a country is to engage in inflationary policies. Such policies benefit debtors at the expense of creditors, and act generally to equalize relative wealth levels. Inflationary policies are particularly attractive in the United States because of the country's large foreign-held debt.[142] Among the many problems with inflation as a way of redistributing wealth is that it can be a political powder keg. The reason is that although inflation improves the relative wealth levels of the poor, it makes them feel worse off in the short term. In the current environment, many people have negative net worth but some cash. Inflation improves their net worth but makes them run out of cash faster. When people are out of cash, out of a job, and out of borrowing power, they hit the streets.

From this perspective, I cannot imagine a worse policy than systematically bailing out large companies that are in trouble. These bailouts are clearly inflationary. At least some of this inflation is anticipated and shows up as a lower dollar, higher oil prices, and higher commodity prices generally. This means that you're transferring money to the rich (the owners of the stocks and bonds of the bailed-out companies), and you're causing

---

[142] Kenneth Rogoff, "Embracing Inflation," Guardian, December 2, 2008, http://www.guardian.co.uk/commentisfree/cifamerica/2008/dec/02/global-economic-recession-inflation (accessed August 16, 2009); Miller, "US Needs More Inflation to Speed Recovery, Say Mankiw, Rogoff."

the poor to run out of cash faster. In the case of an auto bailout, at least people keep their jobs—though arguably at too high a cost. On the other hand, many of the financial bailouts we've seen save few jobs; they are mostly just wealth transfers to the rich.

The psychology of stimulus packages, bailouts, and asset price support programs is deeply, deeply flawed. The word *stimulus* should be interpreted as "intergenerational wealth transfer." The burden for stimulus packages and bailouts will be borne mostly by future generations, as we are borrowing the money to pay for the bailouts. Why should the young be paying to support asset prices? They don't own any assets. A program that successfully uses government funds to prop up house prices hurts them twice: they have to pay higher taxes in expectation, and they will never get a cheap house.

Inflation is a form of wealth tax. It's a hidden transfer from holders of money to printers of money (the government). It's far from ideal in that it transfers wealth in a somewhat random and unfair way, and it's especially harmful to people like widows and retirees who cannot afford to take the risks that inflation-protection investments require. A wealth tax might dominate an inflation tax in that it's a deliberate and controllable policy, and it avoids some of the powder keg effects of inflation mentioned earlier. It counteracts them, in fact, as it makes people feel that the wealthy are suffering a bit in bad times as well.

As a policy objective, "making people feel that the wealthy are suffering" should not rank high. People in other countries have voiced that sentiment in the polls before, with the result that everyone becomes poor. A major problem in the United States now is that legitimacy of wealth has gone way, way down. Excess in the financial sector went parabolic during the past decade. The buoyancy of financial markets from 1980 to 2007 meant huge wealth for those who worked in the industry, for those who invested in financial assets, and for those who supplied the financial assets that were craved (including the market-focused entrepreneurs and venture capitalists of Silicon Valley). The popular view that the financial sector led the US economy into the doldrums, coupled with the litany of financial market scandals (AIG and Madoff were particularly destructive), has hurt the legitimacy of wealth, perhaps irreparably, and it is not too much of a stretch to imagine feelings about the legitimacy of wealth reaching Latin American levels in coming years.

The financial news station CNBC was very often in the background in the scenes of Aaron Sorkin's *The West Wing*. This perhaps had a bit to do with the fact that *The West Wing* appeared on CNBC's parent network, but it was there also because the writers of the show were trying to make a subtle statement about the importance of financial market reaction on the decisions of the executive branch. Needless to say, in the last ten years, there's been no need for subtle statements—the influence of the financial sector on policy has reached a point of absurdity.

In a 2002 interview, notable political commentator Kevin Phillips said, "When is the last time you heard someone in the financial sector say, 'I don't want any help from Alan Greenspan?' Or, 'He should stay the hell out of my life?' They want help from Alan Greenspan and from the Treasury every year for every crisis you can imagine."[143] He went on to note that finance is the "most subsidized, petted, and socialized industry in the United States." Surely even Phillips has been amazed by the aggressiveness of the bailouts and subsidies. Given that credit creation and asset ownership over the past twenty years have been among the most subsidized activities in history, what kind of sense does it make to redistribute based on future

---

[143] David Barsamian, "An Interview with Kevin Phillips," Progressive, September 2002, http://www.thirdworldtraveler.com/Kevin_Phillips/Interview_KevinPhillips.html (accessed August 16, 2009).

income, when those subsidies are likely to decrease dramatically going forward?

People prefer capitalism during good times and socialism during bad times. A 2009 Rasmussen Reports national telephone survey showed that 53 percent of Americans believed capitalism to be better than socialism, 27 percent were not sure which was better, and 20 percent believed socialism was better.[144] In comparison, 70 percent of voters said that free markets were better, while only 15 percent preferred a government-managed economy, and 15 percent were undecided in a poll conducted one year earlier.[145] By 2011, these numbers moved to 68 percent in favor of capitalism, 24 percent for socialism, and the rest undecided.[146]

President Obama was elected partially because people desired to vote themselves wealth. This is true despite the fact that, in both 2008 and 2012, the poorest states showed a strong tendency to vote for Republicans and the richest states showed a strong tendency to vote for Obama.[147] As Robert Frank pointed out in his book *What's Wrong with Kansas?*, many of the nation's poor vote against redistributive policies, either because they think redistribution is bad policy or because their views on social issues are more in line with Republican views.

---

[144] Rasmussen Reports, "Just 53% Say Capitalism Better Than Socialism," http://www.rasmussenreports.com/public_content/politics/general_politics/april_2009/just_53_say_capitalism_better_than_socialism (accessed August 16, 2009).

[145] Rasmussen Reports, "Voters Champion Free Market but Want More Regulation," December 29, 2008, http://www.rasmussenreports.com/public_content/business/general_business/december_2008/voters_champion_free_market_but_want_more_regulation (accessed June 3, 2010).

[146] Rasmussen Reports, "Favorables: Socialism 24%, Capitalism 68%," November 28, 2012, http://www.rasmussenreports.com/public_content/politics/general_politics/november_2012/favorables_socialism_24_capitalism_68 (accessed January 12, 2013).

[147] "State Personal Income 2008," Bureau of Economic Analysis, http://www.bea.gov/newsreleases/regional/spi/2009/pdf/spi0309.pdf (accessed August 16, 2009).

Relative to where we are now, in January 2013, I see the forces pushing us leftward in economic matters as significantly stronger than the forces pushing us rightward. The legitimacy of wealth has been tangibly damaged. It's likely that this process will continue. The liquidity operations and asset price support programs conducted by the Federal Reserve since the start of this financial crisis have resulted, predictably, in an increase in commodity prices and a partial reflation of the equity indexes. In addition, the recent reflation in equity markets has been driven at least as much by an increase in long-term inflation expectations as by expectations of a return of real economic strength. The net result of Federal Reserve policy so far has been a partial, though still quite incomplete, recovery of the net worth of the wealthiest, while the poor and middle class experience downtick after downtick, with seemingly few prospects for a turnaround.

A service economy seems particularly vulnerable to a decline in the legitimacy of wealth. When the difference between the guy driving a luxury car and his valet comes to be seen as simply a matter of luck, connections, and perhaps guile, and class mobility comes to be seen as stifled, I don't see how people can be expected to get along.

The reason I expect a leftward move in politics has nothing to do with merit. I expect a move to the left for political reasons, and I believe it would be mostly disastrous. Daniel Yergin and Joseph Stanislaw's *The Commanding Heights: The Battle Between Government and the Marketplace That Is Remaking the Modern World* tells the story of a worldwide rolling back of government that occurred starting in the early 1980s. To an impressive extent, this rollback in government was driven by the intellectual class. We are seeing a leftward move in politics across most Western countries that is likely to continue, and it is largely against the advice of the intellectual class, for whom the historical and intellectual case against socialist policies remains firmly in mind. For the world at large, cyclically, these matters are just forgotten and must be relearned at repeated intervals. Or perhaps people vote their short- to medium-term personal interest, which for the majority accord with socialist policy for the moment, and they do this regardless of their views about the public interest.

7 THE MACROECONOMICS OF DELEVERAGING

Charles Dickens said of debtors' prisons, "Any one can go IN...but it is not every one who can go out."[148] In today's highly leveraged macroeconomic environment, Dickens's words have found renewed resonance. Current economic circumstances increase the pressures for a period of sustained deleveraging. Deleveraging occurs when debt levels decline relative to a measure of income or assets. The macroeconomic effects of deleveraging are far more severe than most observers appreciate. This chapter supports one of the more controversial theses of this book: that successful, comprehensive deleveraging and long-term US federal government solvency are incompatible.

---

[148] Charles Dickens, Little Dorrit (New York: Penguin, 1998), 112.

The United States has experienced an incredible increase in indebtedness over time. Total debt in nonfinancial sectors to GDP in the United States is at 243 percent as of 2009. GDP in 2009 was $14.256 trillion.[149] This implies a total debt of around $34.702 trillion. The rough breakdown of this is government debt of $10.168 trillion,[150] corporate debt of $10.998 trillion, and household debt of $13.536 trillion.[151] As of December 21, 2012, total debt in nonfinancial sectors to US GDP stands at about 250 percent. Recent best estimates for 2012 GDP sit at $15.88 trillion, implying a total indebtedness of about $39.7 trillion. The nominal indebtedness alone is quite profound, but what is most important is that the debt trend remains post-crisis.

If one is analyzing the world from the perspective of neoclassical economics, then one is flying blind in a world of massive indebtedness. In *Stabilizing an Unstable Economy*, Hyman Minsky notes, "In the neoclassical view, speculation, financing conditions, inherited financial obligations, and the fluctuating behavior of aggregate demand have nothing whatsoever to do with saving, investment, and interest rate determination."[152] Minsky thought that modern economic theory, by abstracting away from institutional realities, missed too much of what is important. I'll take a deeper look at his theories later in this chapter.

---

[149] Congressional Budget Office, The Budget and Economic Outlook: Fiscal Years 2010 to 2020, January 2010, http://www.cbo.gov/ftpdocs/108xx/doc10871/01-26-Outlook.pdf, p. 24 (accessed November 27, 2011).

[150] See Table D-2 of Federal Reserve Statistical Release Flow of Funds Accounts of the United States Flows and Outstandings Fourth Quarter 2009, March 11, 2010, http://www.federalreserve.gov/releases/z1/20100311/z1r-1.pdf (accessed November 27, 2011).

[151] Crown Financial Ministries, Household Debt in 2007, http://www.crown.org/LIBRARY/ViewArticle.aspx?ArticleId=762 (accessed November 27, 2011). The article was adapted from the original articles by Bette Noble, Crown Sr. R&D Specialist.

[152] Hyman Minsky, Stabilizing an Unstable Economy (Columbus, OH: McGraw-Hill, 2008), 123.

The macroeconomic effects of debt are a bit difficult to get one's head around. Debt that is taken on for the purposes of either consumption or investment will tend to increase the money supply in the period it is taken on and decrease the money supply in the period it is paid back. Debt taken on for purposes of consumption will tend to increase GDP in the period of consumption by an amount somewhat greater than the value of the debt, and it will tend to decrease GDP in the period it is paid back.

The ratio of total debt to GDP has trended relentlessly upward for thirty years. This is the basis for George Soros's superbubble hypothesis—simply put, the notion that markets reflect more than the fundamentals would suggest that cause asset prices to move to extremes. The superbubble is not confined to the United States—most Western economies have traveled a similar trajectory. According to Peter Warburton, who examined the performance of major Western economies during this superbubble, "It appears that a given percentage addition to private sector debt is associated with less and less economic growth with the passage of time."[153] There appears to be diminishing short-term macroeconomic returns to debt, and, in the United States, at least, we are far out on the curve.

Roughly speaking, every dollar used to pay off debt in a given period represents a reduction of aggregate demand by one dollar and a reduction of GDP by one dollar. This is counterintuitive but approximately correct. However, our standard economic intuition might suggest that when one dollar is used to pay off debt, some of that dollar will then be spent by the lender, offsetting the direct decrease in aggregate demand; aggregate demand, therefore, could stay somewhat constant. But this logic is wrong. Understand that, at the end of the day, the economy consists only of

---

[153] Warburton, Debt and Delusion, 217.

individuals; government and corporations are both economic constructs that are worthless in the absence of the individuals behind them. A dollar of debt reduction in one period will reduce income, expenditure, and output by a dollar in that period, unless there is a change in individual preferences regarding consumption and saving decisions.

Suppose I have a salary of $100,000, a bank account containing $100,000, and a note receivable that has a market value of $50,000. When choosing how much to spend in the next year, the primary variables of interest are my wealth level, my income level, the real interest rate offered by potential investments, and the value I attribute to future consumption as opposed to current consumption. Whether my wealth takes the form of cash or notes receivable doesn't make much difference. For my $50,000 note receivable to be paid off in a given time period and converted to cash in my account, someone somewhere in the economy will have to have income that exceeds expenditure by at least $50,000 in that period. On some level, I might understand that if I don't increase my expenses by $50,000 in the period that my debt is paid off, then aggregate demand and aggregate output will be light by $50,000 in that period, but I don't much care: my objective is to maximize my individual well-being. If debt repayment occurs en masse, then we can expect a sharp retrenchment in output and expenditure. Corporations can hardly be expected to invest heavily when they see consumption on the retreat. This disconnect between optimal behavior at the aggregate level (full employment and full resource utilization) and optimal behavior at the individual level was emphasized by Keynes. Keynes argued that, at such times, government can borrow and spend to push closer to full resource utilization. The analysis is sound, and his insights have no doubt improved cumulative economic well-being over time, but Keynesian spending of this type does nothing whatsoever to improve an economy's debt-to-GDP ratio; it merely replaces consumer and business indebtedness with government indebtedness. There is a definite sense in which true deleveraging requires some pain.

For an economy with a debt-to-GDP ratio of 150 percent, a 4 percent decline in the debt ratio over one year would imply a 6 percent decline in aggregate demand in the first year, relative to what aggregate demand would have been with stable debt levels. Recall that debt can't change anyone's lifetime budget constraint; it can only move expenditures forward and backward in time. Debt for consumption is often highly rational: there is wisdom in spending while young, when time is plentiful and money is hard to come by, and paying off the resulting loans while old, when time is short and money comes more easily. That said, borrowing for consumption is an altogether riskier proposition, for an individual or for a society, than borrowing for investment. All sectors of the US economy increased borrowing relative to income at a fairly rapid rate over the past thirty years. For every year that cumulative borrowing increased relative to income, that increased borrowing represented an increase in aggregate demand and aggregate output relative to what it would have been if the ratio between borrowing and income had remained constant. That increased expenditure and output, though, comes at a cost—borrowing implies that at some future point expenditure and output must be lower than they would be if there were no debts to repay.

For Peter Warburton, there are only "four resolutions to unmanageable debt." These are: clemency, or to beg forgiveness; bankruptcy, to default on one's obligations; paternalism/socialism, finding a benefactor who will carry the debt for you; and, finally, inflation/debauchery/theft, the debasement the currency in which the debt is measured.[154] It's often better for all parties except the lender to find a

---

[154] Peter Warburton, "Global Credit Perspectives," Economic Perspectives Ltd, June 2009, http://www.economicperspectives.co.uk/fileadmin/resources/Global_Credit_Perspective_June_20

resolution to the debt. Consider a hypothetical economy that is similar to that of the United States in all regards except that all debt must be paid off in full in real terms (this isn't possible, as it precludes personal and business bankruptcy). Suppose that in forty years, both economies have deleveraged from their current debt-to-GDP ratio of 230 percent to a debt-to-GDP ratio of 150 percent. The US economy, which would have alleviated debt through a combination of repayment and the four resolutions cited above, would be infinitely better off than our hypothetical economy, where all debt had to be paid in full. Our hypothetical economy would have a level aggregate output very far below the economy's potential output, simply because debt reduction would act as a significant drag on aggregate demand and aggregate output, year after year, for forty years. The US economy would have a level of output much closer to potential output after forty years; debt would have been a drag on growth, as in our hypothetical economy, but to a much lesser extent, as much of the debt would have been inflated away, negotiated down, or outright ignored.

Much of the debt that we've incurred will in fact be repaid, and this will be a significant drag on US growth, not just for a few years but for a very long time. Rich people and rich institutions carry much of the debt and they have a lot to lose by defaulting—this is why most debt will be paid down. The reason it will be a drag on growth for a long time is that reasonable improvements in the leverage ratios of any major sector of the economy can only occur over long time horizons.

Much of the aggregate US debt, however, will not be repaid, and chief among those debts are those of the US government. Among the primary reasons US government debt will not be repaid is that the macroeconomic consequences of deleveraging are politically untenable. The deleveraging

---

09.pdf, 11 (accessed November 27, 2011).

process hasn't really started—faced with much lower levels of individual and corporate borrowing, the government has decided to make up the difference by increasing its borrowing and spending. There are fairly strong economic arguments suggesting that this is what the government should be doing at this time. My view, however, is that economics is almost beside the point—the political reality is that large-scale deleveraging will never be allowed to occur. Given that individuals and corporations have largely tapped out their ability to borrow, we can expect that the government will continue to borrow and spend at high levels.

Going forward in 2013 and beyond, we have two options: we can start to rein in government spending, which will very likely initiate a debt-deflation process, or we can continue government spending at high levels and risk US government solvency. By risking government solvency, we will experience not a default but rather an unhappy state where the government can only fund itself by having the Federal Reserve create money to buy US Treasury bonds on an ongoing basis. I will consider the first strategy for a moment, but, as mentioned, I regard it as politically impossible.

One merit of allowing the economy to go through a painful debt-deflation process is that it allows the economy to purge itself of debt. As we've seen, an economy that has the capacity to purge itself of debt has better long-term growth potential than one that doesn't. There's value in going through a period of pain where, as it were, the equity that is left in the system is untangled from debt. As this untangling occurs, we will necessarily see distressed sales and lower asset prices, but these lower prices will enable us to see the places in the system where the debt load has become unbearable. These unbearable debt loads will produce bankruptcies or other forms of debt renegotiation, and these processes will allow debt to be removed from the system. Hyman Minsky saw clearly that this debt-deflation process, first suggested by Irving Fisher in the 1930s, would never be allowed to occur in a post–Great Depression world. It is simply too painful.

In *The Holy Grail of Macroeconomics: Lessons from Japan's Great Recession*, Richard Koo suggests that Japan's long recession of the 1990s was a balance sheet recession.[155] Starting in 1989, Japan's debt-fueled bubbles in equity and real estate began a fairly rapid and severe deflation, leaving many individuals and corporations in low or negative equity positions. Koo contends that the weak balance sheets that resulted from the bubble collapse forced individuals and corporations into a regime of debt repayment and low spending.

Japan suffered from the typical ailment of an economy going through a balance sheet recession—a liquidity trap. A liquidity trap results from a shortage of creditworthy borrowers and potentially profitable projects. During a liquidity trap, attempts by the central bank to increase the money supply will result mostly in a buildup of reserves, as we have seen in the United States since 2009. Koo argues persuasively that without massive government borrowing and spending, the retreat in private sector spending would have caused a severe and long-lasting depression. Similar to Minsky, he argues that money supply growth is a borrower-pulled rather than lender-pushed phenomenon, implying that monetary policy is ineffective in an environment with few creditworthy borrowers and profitable projects.

It's clear that the United States and much of the Western world is entering a balance sheet recession of the type that Koo examined. But the economy of the United States now and that of Japan in the 1990s are different in fundamental respects. Japan went into its crisis with a much higher level of national savings and with a much healthier current account. Most observers contend that Japan had a bigger asset bubble and larger

---

[155] Richard Koo, The Holy Grail of Macroeconomics: Lessons from Japan's Great Recession, rev. ed. (Singapore: John Wiley & Sons [Asia] Pte. Ltd, 2009).

debt loads going into the crisis, though this point is arguable. Japan had an easier time funding its desired level of government borrowing and spending because of higher national savings and because, unlike in the crisis today, the Japanese were somewhat alone during most of their economic crisis. The present crisis is unique in its sheer breadth. Not all governments will be able to borrow and spend at the same time. As Peter Warburton puts it, "[T]he difficulty in contemplating a large expansion of public debt lies in the confluence of the ambition."[156]

Richard Koo suggests that the balance sheet devastation in Japan was so severe that Japan's record of low but mostly positive economic growth and relatively stable prices in the last twenty years can be thought of as something of an accomplishment. The headwinds Japan faced were so strong as to make stagnation a good result. Indeed, Koo's analysis suggests that, but for minor missteps, Japanese economic policymakers were remarkably enlightened. It is incredible that Japan's output per capita could be relatively stagnant over a twenty-year period in which technological progress was presumably occurring quite quickly. This is simply a testament to the fact that deleveraging exerts a very strong downward influence on aggregate demand, and aggregate demand constrains the long-term growth rate in output. In the 1980s, Japan was praised for its collective discipline. Twenty years later, there was less talk of Japan's positive attributes, but there's perhaps an underappreciation of the discipline and long-term fortitude required to combat a severe balance sheet recession.

The low-spending, debt deflation option might be more likely to destroy US government finances than the high-spending option. History suggests that the primary source of stress for government finances during times of economic crisis is the shortfall in government revenue, not the increased expenditure associated with bailouts and stimulus programs. The

---

[156] Warburton, Debt and Delusion, 9.

United States has a very progressive tax system, and our businesses use a high amount of operating and financial leverage. If GDP falls a long way, many businesses will have negative income and will pay no taxes or will wind up with negative tax rates.

One reason that a debt-deflation process is politically untenable at present is that it would be fundamentally unfair. What we've experienced for most of the past three decades is a huge borrowing binge that has resulted in a massive run-up of asset prices of all kinds and a monstrous increase in the wealth levels of the wealthiest quartile of Americans. The bottom half hardly improved their standard of living during this time. In a debt-deflation process, the rich would lose a lot of money, to be sure, but the bottom half of Americans would see a crushing decline in living standard.

I believe that the current political environment is such that options involving low levels of government borrowing won't be considered. In 2007, the federal budget deficit was $163 billion (1.2 percent of GDP).[157] The probability that we will bring the deficit below 1.2 percent of GDP in the next twenty-five years is close to zero, for we will be fighting unfavorable demographics and a steep upward trend in entitlement spending. Entitlement spending is around 8.5 percent of GDP but is projected to reach 14.3 percent of GDP by 2030 and 17.9 percent of GDP by 2050.[159]

---

[157] US Department of the Treasury, "Joint Statement of Henry M. Paulson, Jr., Secretary of the Treasury, and Jim Nussle, Director of the Office of Management and Budget, on Budget Results for Fiscal Year 2007," October 11, 2007, http://www.treasury.gov/press-center/press-releases/Pages/hp603.aspx (accessed November 27, 2011).

[159] Heritage Foundation, 2009 Federal Revenue and Spending Book of Charts, http://blog.heritage.org/2009/12/31/top-ten-charts-of-2009/ (accessed November 27, 2011); Congressional Budget Office, The Long-Term Budget Outlook, June 2009, http://www.cbo.gov/ftpdocs/102xx/doc10297/06-25-LTBO.pdf (accessed November 27, 2011).

Any set of policies that would act to increase the overall indebtedness of the individual and the business sectors would be particularly bad in the long term. Yet there's a lot of evidence that we're heading in this direction. The residential real estate market would have seen a much more complete collapse in 2009 without heavy government intervention. The Federal Housing Administration backstopped 19 percent of all new housing loans in the first half of 2009, compared to 2 percent in 2006.[160] A November 2012 report by the FHA's actuarial arm concluded that it lacks the current liquidity to handle losses on its $1.1 trillion mortgage debt pool; future negative cash flows will be negative $39.1 billion on only $25.6 billion in resources.[161] Analysts suggest a taxpayer bailout may be needed to cover the gap. On a larger scale, if the United States effectively backstops all major financial institutions, and then strongly encourages them to lend, they are engaging in a very costly program that encourages increased indebtedness.

To apply a poker analogy, there's a chance that in the United States, rather than undertake a long-term deleveraging process, we will decide to ship it in. This is the unspoken message delivered by policymakers—that we've worked ourselves into a situation where the whole enterprise must be risked; it is only a question of how. This is something akin to the psychology of the rogue trader applied to an entire society. The nature of our gamble would be a leveraged reflation of the economy—a trick that seemed unlikely in the fall of 2008, though we'd pulled it off many times in the past. To understand how a reflation would work, note that a shortage of profitable projects and creditworthy borrowers does not necessarily imply a

---

[160] James Hagerty, "FHA Will Tighten Credit Standards," Wall Street Journal, September 19, 2009, http://online.wsj.com/article/SB125328361187423115.html (accessed November 27, 2011).

[161] Federal Housing Administration, "Actuarial Review Fiscal year 2012," November 2012, http://www.foxbusiness.com/government/interactive/2012/11/15/full-text-fha-audit-for-fiscal-2012/ (accessed January 12. 2013).

liquidity trap. One need only find a way to lend to unprofitable projects and noncreditworthy borrowers. The problem is that private lenders are unlikely to make these loans, implying that they must be explicitly or implicitly backstopped by the government.

To engage in a "ship it in" reflationary process, US policymakers need not only willing lenders (this is easy, for the government can backstop loans), but also willing borrowers. Richard Koo's analysis of the Japanese situation suggests that overindebted businesses and consumers in Japan behaved responsibly and chose the painful course of paying down their debts over a long period. The Japanese central bank flooded the banking system with liquidity—Japan, after all, gave us the term *quantitative easing*[162]—but the liquidity didn't translate into loans to consumers or businesses. A similar liquidity trap is going on now in the United States. My contention, though, is that if the government could convince lenders to lend, then American consumers and businesses might just choose to gamble rather than de-lever, and this might represent a fundamental difference between the Japanese situation and the American situation.

The releveraging process that the United States is attempting implies that real interest rates will not hit their natural levels any time soon. This has been a norm in recent years; money borrowing is a heavily subsidized activity. When interest rates are kept below their natural levels in an attempt to stimulate the economy, money is often invested unwisely or used for excessive consumption. If interest rates hit their natural level, investment and saving are likely to occur safely at high levels of interest rates. In other words, high real interest rates encourage the preservation of capital.

Finance has been called the squeaky wheel of capitalism: as Minsky

---

[162] The term was coined by Richard Werner in reference to Japan's liquidity operations during the 1990s; Richard Werner, "Keizai Kyoshitsu: Keiki kaifuku, ryoteiki kinyu kanwa kara," Nikkei, September 2, 1995.

points out, there's a tendency for a capitalist economy to go through cycles of increasing indebtedness. With all else being equal, increased indebtedness implies lower average credit quality. As the cycle of increasing indebtedness continues, the system increasingly finds itself in crises of credit quality. Naturally, the finance industry increases in size as this cycle of increasing indebtedness plays out. When you get to late stages of the cycle, you have severe crises in credit quality coupled with a large absolute size of the financial sector. This eventually results in macroeconomic disaster, as bad loans decimate a large portion of the capital base of the financial sector.

The risk of reflation as a solution to asset price weakness and consumer, government, and corporate indebtedness is that it will very likely end in a crisis of credit quality. The ongoing subprime crisis is an example of a policy of reflation resulting in a crisis in credit quality, but we are still quite far from the natural limit of a crisis in credit quality. This occurs when nearly everyone in the economy focuses on cash flow levels and gives debt repayment little thought. We might be able to stage a successful reflation, but it will only result in a worse crisis in credit quality down the road. What is the logical limit of the asset meltdown-reflation cycle? We have a preview of this already. The penultimate step entails no creditworthy borrowers but the government; then, even the government becomes uncreditworthy.

I've suggested that the reflationary path that the United States is pursuing is its only politically viable option and perhaps its only economically viable option, in the sense that a full-scale deleveraging would be immediately catastrophic for US government finances, featuring massive and difficult to reverse revenue shortfalls at all levels of government. If the reflationary option, featuring large-scale government borrowing and spending coupled with aggressive monetary measures, is the only option on the table, it's also one that will push US government finances to the breaking point.

ACKNOWLEDGMENTS

I would like to thank my students in the Harvard tutorial, "The US in the World Economy." I refined my thinking on the topics covered in this book over hundreds of hours of conversation with my students in this tutorial. Incidentally, one of my students, Grant Wonders, had the enterprising idea to turn his final paper on Greece into an ebook; last I heard, it had sold four thousand copies and was being used as a textbook at the University of Georgia. I can only hope this book does as well.

My editor on this work was the inestimable Janet Byrne. Her talent is mind-blowing. Janet, I hope you will teach me to write, one correction at a time. For research help at various stages on this long journey, I would like to thank my friends Beau Briggs, Michael Goldfarb, Rob Mrkonich, and Annamaria Vrabrie. The work benefitted from comments at various stages from Vesko Kulev, Pat Dwyer, Scott Wyler, Scott Ferguson, Rod Wong, Roger Hu, David Kovtun, and Aaron Brown.

BIBLIOGRAPHY

Aaron, Henry J. "Prescription Drug Bill: The Good, the Bad, and the Ugly." Brookings Institution. http://www.brookings.edu/articles/2004/0115useconomics_aaron.aspx?rssid=washington+dc (accessed March 27, 2009).

Ahern, William. "Comparing the Kennedy, Reagan and Bush Tax Cuts." Tax Foundation. http://www.taxfoundation.org/news/show/323.html (accessed March 17, 2009).

Amadeo, Kimberley. "US Federal Budget: Mandatory Spending." http://useconomy.about.com/od/fiscalpolicy/p/Mandatory.htm (accessed June 3, 2009).

Amber, David. "Foreign Purchases of US Debt and Equity: Some Stylized Facts." http://www12.georgetown.edu/students/dpa3/doc/bondeq_facts.pdf (accessed March 9, 2009).

"Analytical Perspectives: Budget of the US Government, Fiscal Year 2008." http://www.gpoaccess.gov/usbudget/fy08/pdf/spec.pdf (accessed August 10, 2009).

"Assumptions Used to Project Social Security's Financial Condition." American Academy of Actuaries. http://www.actuary.org/pdf/socialsecurity/assumptions_0104.pdf (accessed August 12, 2009).

Axelrod, Robert. The Evolution of Cooperation. New York: Basic Books, 2006.

Azémar, Céline, and Andrew Delios. "Tax Competition and FDI: The Special Case of Developing Countries." DPRU Conference 2008. http://www.dpru.uct.ac.za/Conference2008/Conference2008_Papers/Celine%20Azemar.pdf (accessed August 18, 2009).

Ball, Douglas B. Financial Failure and Confederate Defeat. Urbana: University of Illinois Press, 1991.

Bank, Steven A., Kirk J. Stark, and Joseph J. Thorndike. War and Taxes. Washington, D.C.: Urban Institute Press, 2008.

Barsamian, David. "An Interview with Kevin Philips." Progressive, September 2002. http://www.thirdworldtraveler.com/Kevin_Phillips/Interview_KevinPhillips.html (accessed August 16, 2009).

Biggs, Andrew G. "Good News on Social Security?" Christian Science Monitor, April 15, 2008. http://www.csmonitor.com/2008/0415/p09s02-coop.html (accessed August 12, 2009).

———. "Wishful Thinking on Social Security." CATO Institute. http://www.cato.org/pub_display.php?pub_id=4481 (accessed August 12, 2009).

Blustein, Paul. And the Money Kept Rolling In (And Out). New York: Public Affairs, 2005.

———. The Chastening: Inside the Crisis That Rocked the Global Financial System and Humbled the IMF. New York: Public Affairs, 2003.

Board of Governors of the Federal Reserve System. "Press Release dated September 13, 2012." http://www.federalreserve.gov/newsevents/press/monetary/20120913a.htm (accessed January 13, 2013).

"Boomer Stats." Baby Boomer Headquarters. http://www.bbhq.com/bomrstat.htm (accessed March 16, 2009).

Bravo, Jorge. "Intergenerational Transfers and Social Protection in Latin America." Paper presented at the Economic Commission for Latin America and the Caribbean, 2005.
http://www.un.org/esa/population/meetings/Proceedings_EGM_Mex_2005/bravo.pdf (accessed June 30, 2009).

Budget of the United States: Historical Tables Fiscal Year 2005. http://www.gpoaccess.gov/usbudget/fy05/hist.html (accessed August 12, 2009).

Budget of the United States Government: Fiscal Year 2010. Summary Tables, Table S-2. Office of Management and Budget.
http://www.whitehouse.gov/omb/assets/fy2010_new_era/Summary_Tables2.pdf (accessed March 7, 2009).

Buffet, Warren. "Buy American. I am." New York Times, October 17, 2008.

Bureau of Economic Analysis. "National Economic Accounts." http://www.bea.gov/national/xls/gdplev.xls (accessed August 10, 2009).

———. "National Income and Product Accounts Table—Table 1.1.1 Percent Change from Preceding Period in Real Gross Domestic Product."
http://www.bea.gov/national/nipaweb/SelectTable.asp?Popular=Y (accessed March 18, 2009).

———. "National Income and Product Accounts Table: Table 1.1.5., Gross Domestic Product." http://www.bea.gov/national/nipaweb/TableView.asp?SelectedTable=5&FirstYear=2007&LastYear=2008&Freq=Qtr (accessed March 25, 2009).

———. "National Income and Product Accounts Tables: Table 5.1. Saving and Investment." http://www.bea.gov/national/nipaweb/TableView.asp?SelectedTable=120&Freq=Qtr&FirstYear=2006&LastYear=2008 (accessed March 27, 2009).

———. "State Personal Income 2008."
http://www.bea.gov/newsreleases/regional/spi/2009/pdf/spi0309.pdf (accessed August 16, 2009).
———. "US International Transactions Account Data."
http://www.bea.gov/international/bp_web/simple.cfm?anon=71&table_id=1&area_id=3 (accessed March 7, 2009).

Bureau of the Public Debt, United States Treasury Department. "Monthly Statement of the Public Debt of the United States: December 31, 2008."
http://www.treasurydirect.gov/govt/reports/pd/mspd/2008/opds122008.pdf (accessed October 27, 2009).

CATO Institute. "Total Federal Revenues: 1900–2003 (Percent of GDP)." http://www.cato.org/research/fiscal_policy/2002/growth1.html (accessed June 2, 2009).

Cauchon, Dennis. "Senor Benefits Costs Up 24%: 'Health Care Crisis' Leads to 8-Year Rise." USA Today, February 14, 2008,
http://www.usatoday.com/printedition/news/20080214/1a_lede14_dom.art.htm (accessed August 12, 2009).

Central Intelligence Agency. "Country Comparison: Public Debt." The World Factbook. https://www.cia.gov/library/publications/the-world-factbook/rankorder/2186rank.html (accessed June 30, 2009).

———. The World Factbook. https://www.cia.gov/library/publications/the-world-factbook/ (accessed August 12, 2009).

———. World Factbook—China. https://www.cia.gov/library/publications/the-world-factbook/geos/ch.html (accessed August 10, 2009).

———. World Factbook—United States. https://www.cia.gov/library/publications/the-world-factbook/geos/us.html (accessed September 29, 2009).

Chait, Jonathan. The Big Con: Crackpot Economics and the Fleecing of America. New York: Houghton Mifflin, 2007.

Chamon, Marcos, and Eswar Prasad. "Why Are Savings Rates of Urban Households in China Rising?" IMF Working Paper. June 2008. http://www.imf.org/external/pubs/ft/wp/2008/wp08145.pdf (accessed August 10, 2009).

Congressional Budget Office. "Capital Gains Taxes and Federal Revenues." http://www.cbo.gov/doc.cfm?index=3856&type=0 (accessed March 17, 2009).
———. "Long-Term Budget Outlook: June 2009." http://www.cbo.gov/ftpdocs/102xx/doc10297/toc.html (accessed October 27, 2009).

Cooper, George. The Origin of Financial Crises: Central Banks, Credit Bubbles and the Efficient Market Fallacy. Petersfield, Great Britain: Harriman House, 2008.

Council on Foreign Relations Blog. http://blogs.cfr.org/setser/2009/06/26/the-2008-us-net-international-investment-position-without-valuation-gains-debt-is-rising/.

"Country Profile: Yemen, August 2008." Library of Congress—Federal Research Division. http://lcweb2.loc.gov/frd/cs/profiles/Yemen.pdf (accessed August 14, 2009).

Csikszentmihalyi, Mihaly. Flow: The Psychology of Optimal Experience. New York: Harper and Row, 1990.

"Data and Trends on Private Giving to Education: Voluntary Support of Education Survey." Council for Aid to Education. http://www.cae.org/content/pro_data_trends.htm (accessed August 18, 2009).

"Debt to the Penny and Who Holds It." TreasuryDirect. http://www.treasurydirect.gov/NP/BPDLogin?application=np (accessed March 27, 2009).

DeNavas-Walt, Carmen, Bernadette D. Proctor, and Jessica C. Smith. "Income, Poverty, and Health Insurance Coverage in the United States: 2007." US Census Bureau. http://www.census.gov/prod/2008pubs/p60-235.pdf (accessed April 17, 2009).

Department of the Treasury and Federal Reserve Board. "Major Foreign Holders of Treasury Securities." http://www.treas.gov/tic/mfh.txt (accessed March 7, 2009).

Dickens, Charles. Little Dorrit. New York: Penguin, 1998.

Domhoff, G. William. "Wealth, Income and Power." http://sociology.ucsc.edu/whorulesamerica/power/wealth.html (accessed August 16, 2009).

Duncan, Richard. The Dollar Crisis: Causes, Consequences, and Cures. New York: Wiley, 2003.

Elkus, Richard. Winner Take All: How Competitiveness Shapes the Fate of Nations. New York:

SETTING SUN: THE END OF U.S. ECONOMIC DOMINANCE

Basic Books, 2008.

Employee Benefit Research Institute. "Do the Social Security Projections Underestimate Future Longevity? Both Job-Based Health Coverage and Uninsured Continue to Rise, CPS Shows." http://www.ebri.org/publications/notes/index.cfm?fa=notesDisp&content_id=3474 (accessed August 12, 2009).

"European Union's Plunging Birthrates Spread Eastward." New York Times, September 4, 2006. http://www.nytimes.com/2006/09/04/world/europe/04prague.html?_r=1 (accessed August 14, 2009).

"Fall of Enron Stock." Encarta. http://ca.encarta.msn.com/media_701610605/the_fall_of_enron_stock.html (accessed March 17, 2009).

Federal Reserve Bank of St. Louis. "FRED Graph: Percent Change Real Gross Domestic Product, Annual." http://research.stlouisfed.org/fred2/graph/?chart_type=line&s[1][id]=GDPCA&s[1][transformation]=pch (accessed July 15, 2009).

Federal Reserve Board. "2007 Survery of Consumer Finances." http://www.federalreserve.gov/pubs/oss/oss2/2007/scf2007home.html (accessed March 27, 2009).

Ferrell, John A. Tip O'Neill and the Democratic Century Boston: Back Bay Books, 2001.

"Florida's Crossroads of Foreclosure and Despair." New York Times, February 8, 2009.

"Forex Reserves Drop for First Time Since 2003." China Daily, December 24, 2008. http://www.chinadaily.com.cn/china/2008-12/24/content_7335345.htm (accessed March 7, 2009).

Fox, Dov. "The Truth about Harvard: A Behind the Scenes Look at Admissions and Life on Campus." Princeton Review, 2004.

Frank, Robert H., and Philip J. Cook. The Winner-Take-All Society: Why the Few at the Top Get So Much More Than the Rest of Us. New York: Penguin, 1995.

Fukuyama, Francis. Trust: The Social Virtues and the Creation of Prosperity. New York: Simon & Schuster, 1996.

"Gaza Strip Total Fertility Rate." Index Mundi. http://www.indexmundi.com/gaza_strip/total_fertility_rate.html (accessed August 14, 2009).

Geithner, Timothy F. "Reducing Systematic Risk in a Dynamic Financial System." Paper presented at the Economic Club of New York, New York City, June 9, 2008. http://www.newyorkfed.org/newsevents/speeches/2008/tfg080609.html (accessed August 18, 2009).

Gelinas, Nicole. "NYC's Debt Disaster." New York Post, September 23, 2008. http://www.nypost.com/seven/09232008/postopinion/opedcolumnists/nycs_debt_disaster_130322.htm (accessed April 17, 2009).

Gifford, Rob. China Road: A Journey into the Future of a Rising Power. New York: Random House,

2007.

Glaser, Philip. "Inflation Versus Deflation: Part Two." http://viewfromthetower.wordpress.com/2008/12/17/inflation-versus-deflation-part-two/ (accessed August 12, 2009).

Glasner, David. Free Banking and Monetary Reform. Cambridge: Cambridge University Press, 1989.

Gleick, James. Faster: The Acceleration of Just About Everything. New York: Pantheon Books, 1999.

Glick, Reuven. "FRBSF Economic Letter, 2008-03: February 1, 2008: 2007 Annual Pacific Basin Conference Summary." Federal Reserve Bank of San Francisco. http://www.frbsf.org/publications/economics/letter/2008/el2008-03.html#5 (accessed August 10, 2009).

Gono, Gideon. Interview: "It Can't Be Any Worse." Newsweek, January 24, 2009. http://www.newsweek.com/id/181221 (accessed August 10, 2009).

"Greed and Fear." Economist, January 22, 2009. http://www.economist.com/members/survery_paybarrier.cfm?issue=20090124 (accessed April 17, 2009).

Greenspan, Alan. "The Challenge of Central Banking in a Democratic Society." Paper presented at the Annual Dinner and Francis Boyer Lecture of the American Enterprise Institute for Public Policy Research, Washington, D.C., December 5, 1996.

Gross, Jane. "Dividing Caregiving Duties, It's Daughters vs. Sons." New York Times, September 23, 2008. http://newoldage.blogs.nytimes.com/2008/09/23/in-the-nursing-home-its-daughters-v-sons/ (accessed August 12, 2009).

Hagan, Joe. "Tenacious G: Inside Goldman Sachs, America's Most Successful, Cynical, Envied, Despised, and (in Its View, Anyway) Misunderstood Engine of Capitalism." New York, July 26, 2009. http://nymag.com/news/business/58094/index1.html (accessed August 18, 2009).

Hagerty, James. "FHA Will Tighten Credit Standards." Wall Street Journal, September 19, 2009. http://online.wsj.com/article/SB125328361187423115.html (accessed October 27, 2009).

Halloway, Grant. "Invisible Enemy Spurs Health Worries." CNN. http://www.cnn.com/2006/HEALTH/conditions/05/09/air.pollution/index.html (accessed August 10, 2009).

Hanke, Steven H. "R.I.P. Zimbabwe Dollar." CATO Institute. http://www.cato.org/zimbabwe (accessed August 10, 2009).

Heritage Foundation. "Current Tax Receipts Below Historical Average." http://www.heritage.org/research/features/budgetchartbook/current-tax-receipts-below-historical-average.aspx (accessed August 12, 2009).

———. "2009 Federal Revenue and Spending Book of Charts," http://www.heritage.org/research/features/BudgetChartBook/ (accessed October 27, 2009).

"Historical Currency Exchange Rates." Oanda.com. http://www.oanda.com/convert/fxhistory (accessed August 5, 2009).

"Household Debt in 2007, Debt and Credit." Crown Financial Ministries. http://www.crown.org/LIBRARY/ViewArticle.aspx?ArticleId=762 (accessed October 27, 2009).

H.R. 1—108th Congress (2003): Medicare Prescription Drug, Improvement, and Modernization Act of 2003. GovTrack.us. http://www.govtrack.us/congress/bill.xpd?bill=h108-1 (accessed Mar 27, 2009).

"Inequality in Income or Expenditure." UNDP Human Development Report 2007/2008. http://hdrstats.undp.org/indicators/ (accessed April 17, 2009).

Infinite Tattoos Blog. http://infinitetattoos.wordpress.com/2008/07/ (accessed August 14, 2009).

Internal Revenue Service. "SOI Tax Stats—Individuals Statistical Tables by Tax Rate and Income Percentile." http://www.irs.gov/taxstats/indtaxstats/article/0,,id=133521,00.html (accessed April 17, 2009).

Ip, Greg. "We're Borrowing Like Mad, Can the US Pay It Back?" Washington Post, January 11, 2009. http://www.washingtonpost.com/wp-dyn/content/article/2009/01/09/AR2009010902325.html (accessed July 15, 2009).

"Is Iceland Facing a Meltdown?" MoneyWeek. http://www.moneyweek.com/news-and-charts/economics/is-iceland-facing-a-meltdown.aspx (accessed August 10, 2009).

"Japan Falls into Spiral of Despair." Sunday Times (London), February 22, 2009. http://business.timesonline.co.uk/tol/business/economics/article5780318.ece (accessed August 14, 2009).

Jiabao, Wen. "Strengthen Confidence and Work Together for a New Round of World Economic Growth." Paper presented at the World Economic Forum 2009, Davos, Switzerland, January 28, 2009. http://online.wsj.com/public/resources/documents/WenJiabao01282009.pdf (accessed March 7, 2009).

"Just 53% Say Capitalism Better Than Socialism." Rasmussen Reports. http://www.rasmussenreports.com/public_content/politics/general_politics/april_2009/just_53_say_capitalism_better_than_socialism (accessed August 16, 2009).

Kadison, Richard, and Theresa Foy DiGeronimo. College of the Overwhelmed: The Campus Mental Health Problem and What to Do About It. San Francisco: Jossey-Bass, 2004.

Kahneman, Daniel, and Amos Tversky. "Prospect Theory: An Analysis of Decision under Risk." Econometrica 47, no. 2 (March 1979).

Kelly, T. D., and G. R. Matos. "US Geological Survey: Gold Statistics." Historical Statistics for Mineral and Material Commodities in the United States: US Geological Survey Data Series 140 (2008). http://pubs.usgs.gov/ds/2005/140/gold.pdf (accessed March 8, 2009).

Kenworthy, Lane. "Tax Myths." http://contexts.org/articles/summer-2009/tax-myths/ (accessed August 18, 2009).

Keynes, John Maynard. The General Theory of Employment, Interest, and Money. New York: Harcourt, Brace, 1936.

Koo, Richard. The Holy Grail of Macroeconomics: Lessons from Japan's Great Recession. New York: Wiley, 2009.

Kotlikoff, Laurence J., and Scott Burns. The Coming Generational Storm. Cambridge: The MIT Press, 2004.

Kotlikoff, Laurence J., Ben Marx, and Pietro Rizza. "Americans' Dependency on Social Security." NBER Working Paper No. 12696, November 2006. http://www.nber.org/papers/w12696 (accessed June 22, 2009).

Kotlikoff, Laurence J., and John N. Morris. "How Much Care Do the Aged Receive from Their Children?: A Bimodal Picture of Contact and Assistance." NBER Working Paper No. W2391, February 1989. http://papers.ssrn.com/sol3/papers.cfm?abstract_id=314627 (accessed June 22, 2009).

Laffer, Arthur B. "The Laffer Curve: Past, Present, and Future." Heritage Foundation. http://www.heritage.org/Research/Taxes/bg1765.cfm (accessed April 17, 2009).

Lerner, Eugene M. "Money, Prices, and Wages in the Confederacy, 1861–1865." Journal of Political Economy 63, no. 1 (1955): 20–40.

Lewis, Michael. The Money Culture. New York: W.W. Norton, 1991.

———. "Wall Street on the Tundra." Vanity Fair, April 2009. http://www.vanityfair.com/politics/features/2009/04/iceland200904 (accessed August 10, 2009).

"Live Births and Birth Rates." InformationPlease Database. Pearson Education Group. http://www.infoplease.com/ipa/A0005067.html (accessed June 22, 2009).

Lodge, David. The Art of Fiction: Illustrated from Classic and Modern Texts. New York: Penguin, 1994.

Luporini, Viviane. "Inflations Adjusted Nominal Deficit: A Note on Robert Barro's Definition." Universidade Federal de Minas Gerais. www.cedeplar.ufmg.br/pesquisas/td/TD%20138.doc (accessed August 12, 2009).

Lyons, Barbara, et al. "The Distribution of Assets in the Elderly Population Living in the Community." The Kaiser Commission on Medicaid and the Uninsured. http://www.kff.org/medicaid/loader.cfm?url=/commonspot/security/getfile.cfm&PageID=53591 (accessed June 22, 2009).

McLean, Bethany, and Peter Elkind. The Smartest Guys in the Room: The Amazing Rise and Scandalous Fall of Enron. New York: Penguin, 2001.

McNeill, J. R., and Paul Kennedy. Something New Under the Sun: An Environmental History of the Twentieth-Century World. New York: W. W. Norton, 2000.

McTeague, Jim. "The Underground Economy: Illegal Immigrants and Others Working Off the Books Cost the US Hundreds of Billions of Dollars in Unpaid Taxes." Wall Street Journal: Classroom Edition, April 2005. http://wsjclassroom.com/archive/05apr/econ_underground.htm (accessed August 18, 2009).

Mezrich, Ben. The Accidental Billionaires: The Founding of Facebook—A Tale of Sex, Money, Genius and Betrayal. New York: Doubleday, 2009.

Miller, Ellen. "When the Tables Were Turned." http://tpmcafe.talkingpointsmemo.com/2005/10/07/when_the_tables_were_turned/ (accessed

August 12, 2009).

Miller, Richard. "US Needs More Inflation to Speed Recovery, Say Mankiw, Rogoff." Bloomberg News Service, May 19, 2009. http://www.bloomberg.com/apps/news?pid=20601109&sid=auyuQlA1IRV8&refer=home (accessed June 8, 2009).

Minsky, Hyman. Stabalizing an Unstable Economy. Columbus, OH: McGraw-Hill, 2008.

Morgenson, Gretchen, and Don Van Natta Jr. "Paulson's Calls to Goldman's Tested Ethics." New York Times, August 8, 2009. http://www.nytimes.com/2009/08/09/business/09paulson.html?pagewanted=4&_r=1&dbk (accessed August 18, 2009).

Morrison, Wayne M., and Marc Labonte. "CRS Report for Congress: China's Holdings of US Securities: Implications for the US Economy." http://fpc.state.gov/documents/organization/99496.pdf (accessed August 10, 2009).

Morris, Charles. Money, Greed, and Risk: Why Financial Crises and Crashes Happen. New York: Crown Business, 1999.

National Alliance on Mental Illness. "Major Depression." http://www.nami.org/Template.cfm?Section=By_Illness&template=/ContentManagement/ContentDisplay.cfm&ContentID=7725 (accessed August 14, 2009).

National Center for Health Statistics. "Health, United States, 2007—With Chartbook on Trends in the Health of Americans." http://www.cdc.gov/nchs/data/hus/hus07.pdf#027 (accessed March 27, 2009).

National Institutes of Mental Health. "Numbers Count: Mental Disorders in America." http://www.nimh.nih.gov/health/publications/the-numbers-count-mental-disorders-in-america/index.shtml (accessed August 14, 2009).

Obama, Barack. "Remarks of President Barack Obama—Address to Joint Session of Congress." Paper presented Tuesday, February 24, 2009. http://www.whitehouse.gov/the_press_office/remarks-of-president-barack-obama-address-to-joint-session-of-congress/ (accessed August 10, 2009).

"Obama, Biden, Governors Meeting Appearance." Huffington Post. http://www.huffingtonpost.com/2008/12/02/obama-biden-governors-mee_n_147710.html (accessed August 18, 2009).

Ofek, Eli, and Matthew P. Richardson. "DotCom Mania: The Rise and Fall of Internet Stock Prices." NBER Working Paper No. W8630, December 2001.

Office of Management and Budget. "Historical Tables: Budget of the United States Government, Fiscal Year 2008." http://www.gpoaccess.gov/usbudget/fy08/pdf/hist.pdf (accessed March 20, 2009).

Ohlemacher, Steven. "AP Enterprise: Federal Tax Revenues Plummeting." Yahoo! News. http://news.yahoo.com/s/ap/us_plummeting_taxes (accessed August 18, 2009).

"Oldest Baby Boomers Turn 60!" US Census Bureau. http://www.census.gov/Press-Release/www/releases/archives/facts_for_features_special_editions/006105.html (accessed

March 17, 2009).

"Olympic Repression and a Gutless IOC: Promises, as Well as Records, Have Been Broken in Beijing." Financial Times, August 15, 2008.

"100 Sexiest Women in the World 2008." FHM, July 2008.

"Open House, Anyone? 1 in 9 Homes Sit Empty." USA Today, April 10, 2009.

Paletta, Damien, and Deborah Solomon. "Geithner Vents at Regulators as Overhaul Stumbles," Wall Street Journal, August 4, 2009. http://online.wsj.com/article/SB124934399007303077.html?mod=rss_com_mostcommentart (accessed August 18, 2009).

Parker-Pope, Tara. "Obesity Rates Stall in US but Stay Stubbornly High," New York Times, January 18, 2012.

Paulson, Henry M. Jr., and Jim Nussle. "Joint Statement of Henry M. Paulson, Jr., Secretary of the Treasury, and Jim Nussle, Director of the Office of Management and Budget, on Budget Results for Fiscal Year 2007." US Treasury Department. http://www.ustreas.gov/press/releases/hp603.htm (accessed October 27, 2009).

Perlstein, Rick. Nixonland: The Rise of a President and the Fracturing of America. New York: Scribner, 2008.

Peter, Laurence J. The Peter Principle: Why Things Always Go Wrong. New York: William Morrow, 1969.

Postman, Neil. Amusing Ourselves to Death: Public Discourse in the Age of Show Business. New York: Viking, 1985.

———. Amusing Ourselves to Death: Public Discourse in the Age of Show Business. 20th Anniversary Edition. New York: Penguin, 2006.

Prante, Gerald. "Summary of Latest Federal Individual Income Tax Data." Tax Foundation. http://www.taxfoundation.org/news/show/250.html (accessed April 17, 2009).

Putnam, Robert. Bowling Alone: The Collapse and Revival of American Community. New York: Simon & Schuster, 2000.

"A Reassessment of How Many Died in the Military Crackdown in Beijing." New York Times, June 21, 1989.

"Remarks by President Bush to Airline Employees, Chicago O'Hare International Airport, Chicago." http://bulk.resource.org/gpo.gov/papers/2001/2001_vol2_1172.pdf (accessed March 16, 2009).

Reinhart, Carmen M., and Kenneth S. Rogoff. This Time Is Different: Eight Centuries of Financial Folly. Princeton, NJ: Princeton University Press, 2009.

Riedl, Bryan M. "A Guide to Fixing Social Security, Medicare, and Medicaid." Heritage Foundation. http://www.heritage.org/research/budget/bg2114.cfm (accessed August 12, 2009).

Rogoff, Kenneth. "Embracing Inflation." Guardian, December 2, 2008.

http://www.guardian.co.uk/commentisfree/cifamerica/2008/dec/02/global-economic-recession-inflation (accessed June 8, 2009).

Rogoff, Kenneth, and Carmen Reinhart. "The Aftermath of Financial Crises." American Economic Review, May 2009.

———. "Banking Crises: An Equal Opportunity Menace." NBER Working Paper No. 14587, December 2008.

Rubin, Harriet. "Ayn Rand's Literature of Capitalism." New York Times, September 15, 2007. http://www.nytimes.com/2007/09/15/business/15atlas.html?pagewanted=1&_r=1 (accessed March 18, 2009).

Setser, Brad. "Chinese Financing of the United States." Paper presented at Roubini Global Economics and the Global Economic Governance Programme, University College, Oxford, England. www.cfr.org/content/meetings/setser.ppt (accessed March 7, 2009).

———. "Read Dean, Areddy and Ng on the management of China's Reserves During the Crisis." RGE Monitor. http://www.rgemonitor.com/globalmacro-monitor/255350/read_dean_areddy_and_ng_on_the_management_of_chinas_reserves_during_the_crisis (accessed August 10, 2009).

Setser, Brad, and Arpana Pandey. "China's $1.7 Trillion Bet: China's External Portfolio and Dollar Reserves." CGS Working Paper, January 2009. http://www.cfr.org/content/publications/attachments/CGS_WorkingPaper_6_China.pdf (accessed August 10, 2009).

Shiller, Robert. Irrational Exuberance. New York: Broadway, 2000.

———. "Thrifty China, Spendthrift America." Project Syndicate. http://www.project-syndicate.org/commentary/shiller40 (accessed August 10, 2009).

Shleifer, Andrei. "Do Demand Curves for Stocks Slope Down?" Journal of Finance 41, no. 3 (July 1996).

Siegel, Jeremy. Stocks for the Long Run. 2nd ed. New York: McGraw-Hill, 1998.

Smith, R. Jeffrey, and Jeffrey H. Birnbaum. "Drug Bill Demonstrates Lobby's Pull: Democrats Feared Industry Would Stall Bigger Changes." Washington Post, January 12, 2007. http://www.washingtonpost.com/wp-dyn/content/article/2007/01/11/AR2007011102081.html (accessed August 12, 2009).

Social Security Administration. "Contribution and Benefit Bases, 1937–2009." http://www.ssa.gov/OACT/COLA/cbb.html (accessed August 12, 2009).

———. "2008 OASDI Trustees Report: Table V.A2-Intermediate Estimates." http://www.ssa.gov/OACT/TR/TR08/V_demographic.html#167717 (accessed March 27, 2009).

Soros, George. The Alchemy of Finance. New York: Wiley, 1994.

———. The New Paradigm for Financial Markets: The Credit Crisis of 2008 and What It Means. New York: PublicAffairs, 2008.

———. "The Theory of Reflexivity." Paper presented at the MIT Department of Economics World Economics Laboratory Conference, Washington D.C., April 26, 1994. http://www.geocities.com/ecocorner/intelarea/gs1.html (accessed March 7, 2009).

"Statistics Iceland." http://www.statice.is/Statistics (accessed August 10, 2009).

Stein, Herbert. "Herb Stein's Unfamiliar Quotations." Slate, May 16, 1997. http://www.slate.com/id/2561/ (accessed March 7, 2009).

Stewart, James B. Den of Thieves. New York: Touchstone, 1992.

Summers, Larry. "The Future of Market Capitalism." Paper presented at Harvard Business School's Global Business Summit, October 14, 2008. http://ksghome.harvard.edu/~lsummer/08.10.16_HBS_Global_Summit_Keynote.pdf (accessed April 17, 2009).

Sussman, Marvin B., Suzanne K. Steinmetz, and Gary W. Peterson, eds. Handbook of Marriage and the Family. New York: Plenum Press, 1999.

Swan, Anna. "Tattoo Statistics." Associated Content. http://www.associatedcontent.com/article/31975/tattoo_statistics.html?cat=7 (accessed August 14, 2009).

Szabo, Liz. "Number of Americans Taking Antidepressants Doubles." USA Today, August 3, 2009. http://www.usatoday.com/news/health/2009-08-03-antidepressants_N.htm (accessed August 4, 2009).

Tax Foundation. "Property Tax on Owner-Occupied Housing, by County, Ranked by Property Taxes as a Percentage of Home Vale, 2005–2007 Average." http://www.taxfoundation.org/taxdata/show/24051.html (accessed April 17, 2009).

———. "State Individual Income Tax Rates, 2000–2009." http://www.taxfoundation.org/taxdata/show/228.html (accessed April 17, 2009).

———. "US Federal Individual Income Tax Rates History, 1913–2009." http://www.taxfoundation.org/taxdata/show/151.html (accessed April 17, 2009).

Tax Policy Center. "Historical Federal Receipt and Outlay Summary." http://www.taxpolicycenter.org/taxfacts/displayafact.cfm?Docid=200 (accessed August 18, 2009).

"Tax Rates Around the World." Worldwide-Tax.com. http://www.worldwide-tax.com/index.asp#partthree (accessed August 16, 2009).

"Tax Year 2007 New York City Personal Income Tax Rates." NYC Finance 2009. http://www.nyc.gov/html/dof/html/services/business_tax_nys_income.shtml (accessed April 17, 2009).

"Theme Parks See Crowds After Attacks." Washington Post, September 22, 2001.

"Timothy Leary." University of Virginia. http://www2.lib.virginia.edu/exhibits/sixties/leary.html (accessed August 18, 2009).

"Top US Marginal Income Tax Rates, 1913–2003." truthandpolitics.org. http://www.truthandpolitics.org/top-rates.php (accessed March 17, 2009).

US Bankruptcy Court: Southern District of New York. "Enron Corp. Bankruptcy Information." http://www.nysb.uscourts.gov/enron.html (accessed March 16, 2009).

US Budget, Fiscal Year 2009, Summary Tables. http://www.gpoaccess.gov/usbudget/fy09/pdf/budget/tables.pdf (accessed August 16, 2009).

US Census Bureau. "Annual Estimates of the Population by Sex and Five-Year Age Groups for the United States: April 1, 2000 to July 1, 2007." http://www.census.gov/popest/national/asrh/NC-EST2007-sa.html (accessed March 27, 2009).

———. "Domestic Net Migration in the United States: 2000 to 2004." http://www.census.gov/population/www/socdemo/migrate.html#estproj (accessed August 12, 2009).

———. "Geographical Mobility: 2006 to 2007 Detailed Tables." http://www.census.gov/population/www/socdemo/migrate/cps2007.html (accessed August 12, 2009).

———. "Population Finder." http://factfinder.census.gov/servlet/SAFFPopulation?_submenuId=population_0&_sse=on (accessed March 25, 2009).

———. "Resident Population Plus Armed Forces Overseas—Estimates by Age, Sex, and Race: July 1, 1955." http://www.census.gov/popest/archives/pre-1980/PE-11-1955.pdf (accessed March 25, 2009).

———. "State and County QuickFacts: Huntsville (city), Alabama." http://quickfacts.census.gov/qfd/states/01/0137000.html (accessed August 14, 2009).

———. "Statistical Abstract of the United States: 2003—Table 83 'Live Births, Deaths, Marriages, and Divorces: 1950 to 2001.'" http://www.census.gov/prod/2004pubs/03statab/vitstat.pdf (accessed August 12, 2009).

———. "US Trade in Goods and Services—Balance of Payment (BOP) Basis." http://www.census.gov/foreign-trade/statistics/historical/gands.pdf (accessed March 19, 2009).

US Department of Health and Human Services. "Statistics Related to Overweight and Obesity." http://www.win.niddk.nih.gov/publications/PDFs/stat904z.pdf (accessed August 14, 2009).

"US's Debtor Status Worsens Dramatically." Washington Times, June 27, 2009.

US Federal Reserve. "Balance Sheet of Households and Non-Profit Organizations." http://www.federalreserve.gov/releases/Z1/current/z1r-5.pdf (accessed August 10, 2009).

"US Tax Laws and Tax System." Worldwide-Tax.com. http://www.worldwide-tax.com/us/us_taxes.asp (accessed August 16, 2009).

Warburton, Peter. Debt and Delusion: Central Bank Follies That Threaten Economic Disaster. Princeton, NJ: WorldMetaView Press, 2005.

———. "Global Credit Perspectives." Economic Perspectives Ltd. http://www.economicperspectives.co.uk/fileadmin/resources/Global_Credit_Perspective_June_2009.pdf (accessed October 27, 2009).

Weidenmier, Marc. "Money and Finance in the Confederate States of America."

http://eh.net/encyclopedia/article/weidenmier.finance.confederacy.us (accessed August 10, 2009).

Weitz, Eric D. Weimar Germany: Promise and Tragedy. Princeton, NJ: Princeton University Press, 2007, 135.

Werner, Richard. The New Paradigm in Macroeconomic: Solving the Riddle of Japanese Macroeconomic Performance. New York: Palgrave Macmillan, 2005.

———. "Keizai Kyoshitsu: Keiki kaifuku, ryoteiki kinyu kanwa kara." Nikkei, September 2, 1995.

"When a Lot of Money Is Bad." Financial Gazette (Zimbabwe). http://www.fingaz.co.zw/index.php?option=com_content&view=article&id=351:when-a-lot-of-money-is-bad&catid=32:companies-a-markets&Itemid=47 (accessed August 10, 2009).

Wines, Michael. "China's Leader Says He Is 'Worried' Over US Treasuries." New York Times, March 13, 2009. http://www.nytimes.com/2009/03/14/business/worldbusiness/14china.html?_r=1 (accessed August 10, 2009).

Wolf, Martin. Fixing Global Finance. Baltimore: Johns Hopkins Press, 2008.

Wolff, E. N. Changes in Household Wealth in the 1980s and 1990s in the US (2004). Unpublished manuscript.

"World Economic Outlook: October 2008." International Monetary Fund. http://www.imf.org/external/pubs/ft/weo/2008/02/weodata/index.aspx (accessed August 10, 2009).

"UNData-Chinese Cities' Populations." United Nations. http://data.un.org/Data.aspx?q=china+cities+population&d=POP&f=tableCode%3a240%3bcountryCode%3a156 (accessed August 10, 2009).

"United States of America: Demography and Population: Total Fertility Rate (2009)." The Henry J. Kaiser Foundation. http://www.globalhealthfacts.org/country.jsp?c=223&i=89&cat=7 (accessed August 14, 2009).

We, Yangfeng. "Overweight and Obesity in China." BMJ, 2006: 333, 362–63. http://www.bmj.com/cgi/reprint/333/7564/362.pdf (accessed August 14, 2009).

"WHO Country Reports: Mental Health: Suicide Prevention and Special Programmes." World Health Organization. http://www.who.int/mental_health/prevention/suicide/country_reports/en/index.html (accessed August 14, 2009).

Yoo, Peter S. "Age Distributions and Returns of Financial Assets." Federal Reserve Bank of St. Louis. http://research.stlouisfed.org/wp/1994/94-002.pdf (accessed August 12, 2009).

Zhao, Rui. "Money, Price and Output." https://netfiles.uiuc.edu/ruizhao/www/econ563/Lecture4_fiscal_theory_of_price.pdf (accessed August 12, 2009).

Zhang, Yin, and Guanghua Wan. "National Savings and Balanced Growth: China vs. India." World Bank. http://siteresources.worldbank.org/INTDECABCTOK2006/Resources/Yin_Zhang&Guanghua_Wan.ppt (accessed August 10, 2009).

Made in the USA
Charleston, SC
02 April 2013